WORKING FOR LONDON'S BUSES

Stories from those involved

LONDON
BUS
MUSEUM

Capital Transport

Illustrations were kindly supplied by the following:

John Barry and TfL   106-113 top
Peter Batty   126, 128 left
Capital Transport   Cover, 6, 22 bottom, 32, 35, 37, 38, 39, 43, 73, 84 bottom, 93 all, 104, 113 bottom, 124, 125
Norman Cohen   127, 128 right
Mike Harris   9, 15, 21, 22 top, 23 both, 25 both, 26, 27, 40, 42, 55 both, 63 top, 67 top, 68, 74 top, 94, 98
Emma Hignett   102, 103
Jedco Product Designers   86, 87, 88, 89, 91, 92
Stephen Jolly   67 bottom
Norman Kemp   58
Chris Leadbeater   83 bottom right
Richard Lewis   56, 59, 60, 61
London Transport Museum   7, 10, 11, 33, 72, 84 top
Pentagram   85
Malcolm Randles   74, 75
Geoff Rixon   29
Doug Rose   Cover drawing, 76-82, 83 left, 114-123
Colin Stannard   4, 12, 13, 14, 16, 17, 19
Ray Stenning   63 bottom, 64, 65
Roger Torode   44, 45, 46, 47, 48, 52, 53
Matthew Wharmby   101, 105

First published 2021

Published by Capital Transport Publishing Ltd
www.capitaltransport.com

ISBN 978 1 85414 460 7

Printed by Parksons Graphics Pvt. Ltd.

Contents

Mercedes bendy bus EA 11051 is seen in Southall on one of the routes for which the vehicles were ideal. Their early disappearance by mayoral decree was for some a cause for celebration and for others a matter of regret.

Title Page: Leyland Olympian L 35 stands in Bexleyheath Broadway on 21 March 1987 to publicise the Autocheck ticketing system trial which started the next day, covering the Thamesmead area and using tickets compatible with the Underground Ticketing System. The bus was one of 260 Olympians delivered in 1986/7 with a new entrance layout for two-stream boarding and a lower step for the right-hand stream following research by Ogle Design.

FOREWORD

London as a great city has always had a bus network to be proud of; many more people than those of us who admit to being enthusiasts regard the London bus as the defining symbol of London, alongside the roundel and the Johnston typeface, and frequently all three together.

Beyond the vehicles and the routes, both always evolving over time as London has evolved, are the operating methods, the organisational structures, the effects of economics and politics, and the extraordinary variety of people who had and have worked on the buses and provide the service daily. And all those subjects are as interesting as the hardware and the evolution of the network.

Here, in a brilliantly original set of essays, are details from those with intimate knowledge about aspects of the operation which will be fascinating if you're reading them as a bystander and compelling if you know the subject, even if you thought you knew it well.

They tell you of the changing fortunes of a monolithic organisation, very much with a military base, as it evolved through economic and political changes, into the mixed economy of today's London Buses. And of the effects on the people who worked for the organisation, and others outside it, and of aspects of the operation which are vital but largely unseen.

Some things written in this book aren't reconcilable with others, because the transformation from the old London Transport to the modern London Buses, as part of TfL, involved fragmentation, experimentation, and commercial and personal risks, which didn't always come off as expected.

But therein lies the fascination – a changing picture of the way London's Buses operate, but always with the intention, at least, of a public service at the heart of our city taking millions to work, school, and play and without which the metropolis wouldn't work well, or at all.

This book is rich on detail, personal and technical, which sets it apart from many worthy but dry histories of vehicles, routes and garages. Everyone who reads it will know more than they did about how London's buses work and how they've evolved.

And no one will be less appreciative of the daily miracle of operating one of the world's largest bus networks as a result of reading this book. It might not be perfect, given the money available and the age of the city's road infrastructure and the competing demands on the limited space it has, but in fact it's a very comprehensive service using modern technology, and still with vocationally committed people, and certainly better than it was when I started with London Transport nearly 50 years ago.

I hope you enjoy reading this book as much as I have; and, even better, Capital Transport, the publisher, has generously agreed to donate all the profits from the sale of it to the London Bus Museum at Brooklands in Surrey. There you will find not only examples of many of the vehicles and hardware referred to, but also more stories of London bus operation like these.

Sir Peter Hendy CBE
Former Commissioner, Transport for London 2006-2015

1 DRIVER TRAINING
Tony Read

The 1960s/70s was a period of full employment and this chapter is set in that period. Bus and coach driving involves long hours and shift work and the demand for drivers far exceeded the supply. Recruiting good staff was a constant challenge for most operators. Training and familiarisation differed considerably between the private sector – mainly the coach industry and the publicly owned bus companies. Obtaining a Public Service Vehicle (PSV) driving licence could take less than two days in the coach sector with virtually no job familiarisation provided afterwards. London Transport ran a 21 day training scheme for the same purpose and additionally there was time for training on different vehicle types and more time for route familiarisation before drivers entered service.

In 1966 I discovered that Grey Green, the largest coach operator in North London, offered training to obtain a PSV driving licence. The instruction was from a very helpful driver, but as I had only driven cars or vans before there is only so much that can be learned in a day and on the PSV test I just about scraped through. The only vehicle familiarisation for my first job was "Always use first gear with this type of vehicle". The coach allocated was a Leyland Leopard. It was nothing like the Bedfords that I had driven during the training. It had a 'crash' gearbox which required the double declutching technique to change gear. Failure to synchronise road and engine speed precisely for each gear change enlightens the novice as to the derivation of the term 'crash'!

In 1969 I accepted a job managing a coach company in North London with work for all of its 20 vehicles. With only seven full time drivers the job was challenging. In 1971 I attended the Road Transport Industry Training Board (RTITB) course for PSV driving instructors, and as a result trained several new drivers. This really helped to alleviate the driver shortage. The RTITB provided an excellent course that served the industry very well. The Thatcher government sadly abolished all of the industry training boards.

RTW 10 on the skid pan at Chiswick works in 1966.

After five years I took a job managing another coach company which I did not enjoy and therefore applied to London Transport (LT) as a bus driver in 1974 (coincidentally the year that LT employed its first female bus driver). At the interview the only question asked was "Are you staying if we give you this job?". This was clearly a reflection of the full employment situation. LT was facing a losing battle to recruit and retain staff.

I reported to the Chiswick Training School for my induction. Many of the senior instructors were ex-forces and Second World War veterans. The school was run like a military establishment. The unfortunate person next to me was having difficulty filling in the forms. He was berated by the sergeant major type instructor standing over him, telling him that if he thought he was going to drive a bus that afternoon he had better wake his ideas up! After lunch I drove an RT bus for the first time. Compared with coaches it was short, tall and narrow and people at bus stops kept putting their hands out. I soon got used to the pre-selector gearbox. I could have taken my test after a day or so but the LT training system was so inflexible that everybody had to go through the full 21 day course, irrespective of their experience. On my third day the LT Chief Examiner had to be driven to North Weald aerodrome to observe London Transport's second woman driver on the LT training track. He asked my instructor why I was not on test yet! However, I still had to complete the full course.

This training mock-up of a driver's cab was constructed, as the 'fleet number' suggests, in 1962 and was kept at Chiswick.

Life as a Driving Instructor at the Chiswick Training School

I was a driver at Muswell Hill garage. Most of my time was spent driving DM, SMS and RML buses. I was appointed as a driving instructor based at Chiswick in 1978. The instructor training was very good and comprehensive. Most of the time was spent on practical work with experienced instructors, all of whom were good at passing on their skills. There were some classroom sessions including assessments for Highway Code knowledge. Commentary driving and identification of deliberate driving mistakes by a senior instructor were also part of the course.

I was allocated RT 4712 as my training bus, which is now the LT Museum's gold RT, and a place to park it at Finchley garage. Although the driver training was administered from Chiswick, instructors worked from all areas of London and would find the most convenient garage with some spare overnight parking capacity to work from. The training buses were all allocated to various garages around the fleet for engineering purposes and had to be taken to their home garage for servicing, or 'rotas' as they are known. Instructors became adept at ingratiating themselves with the engineering staff both at the bus's home garage and at the garage where they parked. Not only did you need to get your bus back from 'rota' promptly, but there were small day-to-day jobs such as a boost start in the morning for a flat battery. RT 4712 was allocated to Potters Bar. Engineering foreman Dougie was very good at playing practical jokes and keeping a straight face. On one occasion my trainee was reversing the bus into a parking space where it was to be left for its 'rota'. Reversing procedure was that it had to be done slowly without touching the throttle. Dougie was walking backwards with the bus and had engaged me in conversation and, unseen by me or the trainee, had his hand up between the radiator and the mudguard and was 'blipping' the throttle lever. This resulted in the bus' kangarooing' in to its parking spot. I rebuked the trainee for using the throttle, who protested that he wasn't touching it. At that point Dougie grinned in his characteristic way! RT 4712 was pristine compared with most training buses. Garage engineers were all asked to recommend an RT for preservation and Dougie submitted RT 4712, which is how it became part of the LT Museum fleet.

Despite the staff shortages London Transport were very particular about references. Applicants needed to be able to account for their career history without unexplained gaps. Any lying or deception discovered would result in training being discontinued. I was sometimes asked to take a trainee back to Chiswick immediately, for them never to be seen again.

Trainees would be picked up on their first day following their initial induction. Over a cup of tea in the canteen (not bought by the Instructor) an assessment would be made of the trainee's experience. They might get a drive round a circuit in Chiswick Works, passing very neglected prototype RM1 each time. Instructors had a maximum of two trainees each. It was challenging if one was at the end of the course and the other was a beginner. The experience of the new trainee could range from a conductor who had never driven, to people with car or van experience or existing HGV or PSV licence holders, including re-engagements - ex LT bus drivers. Some trainees were engineering staff who would not take a PSV test but would still go through the same training as PSV candidates.

The first progress check was designed to assess capability in handling the vehicle competently and driving in light suburban traffic. Conducted by a senior instructor it usually took place after about 10 days in training. It was during this first stage that elements of being a good London bus driver were taught. This meant how to drive safely, smoothly and yet keep up with the traffic. Planning and reading the road were the key elements. Whereas most trainees passed there was a significant minority who were unable to pass this test or in some cases even progress beyond basic steering. Mostly this applied to conductors with provisional driving licences. For them it was endless driving along the A30, and the A4, trying to keep within the road markings without hitting the kerb or drifting in to the lane to the right.

The next stage in the training was Central London – how to drive confidently round Hyde Park Corner, Hammersmith Broadway and many other gyratory systems as well as dealing with heavy traffic in narrow roads, culminating in a second progress check. Some trainees would have their training terminated at this point. For the successful ones the PSV test would follow in a few days. Test details were posted some time in advance. Morning tests would start near the home garage and end at Chiswick with the reversing exercise. Afternoon tests would start at Chiswick with the reversing and often end near the home garage.

Some examiners had favoured routes. For example one would often use Richmond, and another Fulham. It was possible to practise on the likely routes and point out the particular examiner's likes and dislikes. For example one would always ask a particular aspect of the Highway Code and another would be particularly fussy about a mirror check in a particular place. There were also particular places where certain procedures had to be followed. For example, being in third gear by the time you reached the sand box in Church Street, Kensington.

As far as local roads are concerned – they could be anywhere. To alleviate boredom I used to have the bus map open beside me and go somewhere new each day. I think I tried most of the canteens in the fleet for lunch at some point. One needed to be alert however as on one occasion I took a road in Kingston and noticed that only one route used it. When I saw that a bus coming the other way was a single deck RF I knew what that meant and we had to do a three point turn in front of the low railway bridge shortly afterwards.

A common problem was 'test nerves' and although trainees knew how to drive correctly they could be intimidated by the occasion, slow right down and be over cautious. Virtually all first time failures settled

Driver training 'on the road' with RMC 1489 at Turnham Green in March 1981.

Take a great future in both hands
...as a Bus Driver

- Good pay ● Job security
- First class training for men & women
- Free travel on London Transport
  bus and train services

Phone 01-402 0011

Or call at London Transport:
Griffith House, 280 Old Marylebone Road, NW1.
Manor House, Seven Sisters Road, N4.
Chiswick Works, 566 Chiswick High Road, W4.

A recruitment poster for bus interior use dating from 1977.

down for a second test and delivered what was required. Sometimes PSV tests were discontinued because of exceptionally heavy traffic or bad weather. Instructors with morning tests and two passes were rewarded with an early day!

The examiners were all DMIs or Divisional Mechanical Inspectors, their principal roles being to attend serious accidents and to arbitrate in cases of mechanical fault allegations by drivers. A group of DMIs were trained as driving examiners and acted under delegated authority from the Commissioner of Police to conduct PSV driving tests. They could also issue full car licences in the case of conductors who only had a provisional licence. They took this delegated authority very seriously and if anything were over strict. In the case of provisional licence holders the test would last well over an hour, whereas the usual PSV test would be about 45 minutes. Because of internal recruitment and promotion policy DMIs had all been London bus drivers.

Tales of strange and amusing events occurring on test or in training abound, although nothing dramatic occurred to me during my time as an instructor. There was anecdotal evidence of trainees treating the instruction 'Straight over at the roundabout' literally. One examiner told me that a candidate tried to drive across Kew Green rather than round it! This examiner was not unlike Roger Moore in build and had been chosen as his double and stunt driver in the bus scenes in the James Bond film 'Live and Let Die'. He had spent a wonderful few weeks filming in Jamaica.

Amusing little episodes could occur during tests. For example one of my less capable trainees when being tested on the Highway Code was asked:- "Where should you not park your motor vehicle or let it stand?" to

which the reply was:- "'Ell of a lot of places as it 'appens" to which the examiner's response was:- "I know that. I just want you to tell me a few of them."

Trainees were of many different types and I found that age and experience were no guarantees of success. Discovering that my next trainee was a 55 year old lorry driver with 30 years experience would not fill me with confidence. It was often very difficult to break such people of bad habits, so there may be several days of 'unlearning'. Young receptive trainees with little experience could often progress well as they only knew what I had taught them.

I tried to make the training enjoyable and would sometimes set challenges for fun. For example, anybody touching a kerb would buy teas for all or even lunch! Only perfect positioning would enable a left turn from Sydney Street in to the Kings Road without the rear wheels going over the kerb. It caught most people out and I never bought the teas when we took that route!

Sometimes there were other interesting breaks away from basic training. There was an MB class bus converted into an interview office. The instructor would take it daily to where it was to be parked for a week's local recruitment drive. An official would drive a dual control car to the site. He or she would conduct interviews in the bus and the instructor would conduct driving assessments with the car to establish whether the candidate was trainable as a bus driver. On my first assessment I had not realized that the dual controls operated on both sides of the car. The unfortunate candidate was trying unsuccessfully to press the clutch to engage gear. My foot was under the clutch on my side. The pain was considerable! I calmly asked him to take his foot off the clutch and try again. The foot was bruised for some days!

Descriptions of Chiswick would not be complete without mention of the famous skid patch, which was operated by specially trained instructors. The first part of the session was to demonstrate cadence braking – done automatically these days by ABS. This involved driving as fast as possible on to the skid patch – about 28mph and braking hard in a straight line The exercise was repeated but this time applying and releasing the brake as quickly as possible, thus demonstrating the decreased braking distance that could be achieved. The next exercise was to demonstrate that steering is ineffective while the wheels are locked. The trainee would drive on to the skid patch again and this time was instructed to put his hands and feet underneath the driving seat while the instructor by use of the handbrake and the steering wheel put the bus in to a sideways skid – effectively a handbrake turn. The trainee was then told to regain control of the vehicle. The steering did not work as the trainee would instinctively brake and try to straighten the vehicle up to no avail. The next time he had to repeat the exercise but this time leave the brakes alone and straighten the bus up first and then cadence brake.

A length of wood was used to hold the sliding cab door shut, but one of the instructors tended not to use it if he had taken a dislike to the trainee. This resulted in water fountaining into the cab! The most common problem that occurred was that trainees would not drive on to the skid patch fast enough. Anecdotally one instructor had jammed a reluctant trainee's leg on to the throttle only to discover that the leg was wooden. His brother had apparently attended the medical examination on his behalf!

In 1984 I was accepted on to the LT management training scheme. One of my attachments was to the Chiswick Training School where my previous experience gave me insight into how I could suggest procedural improvements. While I was there the instructors were told that the Training School was to be closed. This marked the end of a well known and respected institution which had been very effective at delivering a high standard of training, although it could have been more efficient and productive. The instructors and the functions were devolved to the new bus districts.

I spent the rest of my career in management roles for London's buses and London Underground and working as an independent management consultant. Since retiring I have driven vintage buses for the LT Museum, and have been reunited with RT 4712 after a break of over 35 years!

Bus driver training with another simulator at Chiswick Works in 1975. The first female bus driver had started work for London Transport the year before.

2 FROM DESK TO DRIVER'S CAB
Colin Stannard

It was during our last year at school that the late Bill Cottrell and I responded to an advertisement to join the West London Omnibus Society, which we thought would be something like LOTS is today. We were somewhat shocked to find that it was nothing of the kind and was in fact being initiated by one David Bosher who was the same tender age as us. Bill and I were asked to help him form a club to study London buses and whilst we thought it to be some sort of fantasy, we went along with the idea. Nevertheless, it developed into a wider organisation which changed its name to LOTS, with yours truly as member No.6. I shall never forget running off the first newssheet (a one-pager!) on our school's Banda machine. Perhaps more alarming was the second issue produced on the Gestetner machine we purchased which spat its ink randomly all over Bill's mother's kitchen. Other arrangements were made for housing the machine thereafter. The formation of LOTS came at a time when I had to decide what to do with my career. I yearned to drive buses and despite my Mum's advice, I applied to London Transport for opportunities. I was aware that you could not then drive until the age of 21, so I accepted a junior clerical post at the Traffic Audit office which was spread across four huts alongside Hillingdon Station. There is now just 'my' hut in isolation on the site and I know not what it is used for now. The other three huts were lost when the A40 was diverted through part of the site and the station was also realigned in the 1990s. When I die, maybe someone will attach a blue plaque to its door with the inscription "On 1 September 1964, a 16-year old Colin Stannard started his LT career in this hut".

A higher-grade clerk some 10 years my senior showed me around on my first day and taught me an important lesson there and then. When he showed me the gents toilet, he immediately kicked open all the cubicle doors. When asked why this dramatic display had taken place, David said that "once you confirm there is nobody sitting in any of the 'traps', you can talk about anyone without the danger of being heard."

There was an enormous female population working in the huts checking cash total sheets received from every conductor every day. They all seemed content and happy chatting as they worked, tapping their figures into their manual calculators. One result of this task was to issue a 'shorts and overs' list to the garage where under or overpayments needed to be adjusted by the conductors involved. After having the audacity to tell the supervisor that I was bored, immediately receiving the retort "Bored laddie ? !!!" (Anyone under the age of about 25 was 'laddie' in those days), I did get moved to another job, this time at Griffith House. It was to add up lost mileage returns from each garage so that the grand total could be deducted from the mileage scheduled to be operated to then calculate the cost of the actual daily tyre mileage that LT had to pay. Bus tyres were never purchased then but rented from the tyre company and charged on the basis of their use. Whilst I still sought departure into more interesting work, I did meet some colourful characters there, both called Ernie. One was the first cynic I had encountered who agreed with me that the job was tedious, but hey, they do actually pay you every month and nobody works their socks off for it. The other Ernie had a number of private enterprises he undertook during lunch hours and sometimes in the firm's time which involved trading in quantities of watches and other saleable items. On occasions he took me along for the ride and I met a number of ripe personnel, some of whom worked on LT and others that were really quite shady and did not. My further cries of boredom perhaps nudged the cynical Ernie to have me transferred to the operations staff section at 55 Broadway, which he thought might bring me closer to operations and my eventual hope of becoming a bus driver.

This new post involved me in ordering staff uniforms, monitoring sickness and keeping a set of cards for every new recruit and passing into archives any cards

The Traffic Audit office near Hillingdon station, where I first worked as junior clerk.

for staff who left. Again, a mundane task, although this was another office was full of interesting characters all of whom would go for haircuts from time to time on the grounds that hair grows in the firm's time, so it should also be cut in their time too. In the 'ivory tower', there were numerous other departments and in 1966, at the last run of the RTWs from Brixton garage, I met someone who worked in the bus schedules section. I had lunch with him at work the following week and met some of his colleagues, most of which were avid transport enthusiasts. Up to then, I had not met other enthusiasts within the offices, apart from one Mike Beamish who was another 'laddie' at Hillingdon for some of the time I was incarcerated there. We did not work together for very long, but he joined LOTS and we remained in contact as friends for decades thereafter. What he did warn me about was that it was not always a good idea to be open about transport enthusiasm to people at work. The schedules office seemed to be the totally opposite of that school of thought and at Christmas time they even strung decorations across the ceiling in a pattern which mimicked trolleybus overhead.

In 1966 I was interviewed by a man who I came to know as Gus and I moved into a large office in Chiswick Works. As an enthusiast, it took some time to get over the thrill of actually working in this mecca of the bus world where I could see buses on the skid pan every day. Not only that, but at the other end of the section I worked on were the team who initiated bus movements between garages, and produced daily bus allocation variation sheets. My job was not directly involved in that activity and it has to be said that maybe I didn't put as much effort into it as I should have, but spent too much time chatting with the late Peter Aldridge about his work on bus movements.

There seemed to be two supervisors on my section – not two Ernies but this time two Bills. A custom here and indeed common throughout all LT then was that of drinking. The two Bills and others would disappear about 11.30 to a local pub and not return until about 3.30. On their return, it was funny to watch one of the Bills manually start to cast a list of numbers from the top of a sheet of paper yet never reach the end due to falling asleep slumped across his desk where he remained in that state until time to go home.

I had to compile a weekly report for Mr Shave, a chief engineering manager. This involved another new adventure in that it had to be typed up, which caused me to visit the typing pool – a thrill for any 18-year old 'laddie'! Another advantage of working in the Rolling Stock Office at that time was that along with 11 other people, I managed to arrange purchase for preservation of RTW 467, the last of its type to run in service in May 1966. Also, helped by my current employment, I was able to secure a parking place at reasonable rent for our

The route survey van I drove as part of my second office job, this time based at 55 Broadway.

bus in Fulwell garage. Furthermore, it was three years later that I met my wife Joyce on a trip in RTW 467. She was a friend of the sister of one of our members who had come with us for a trip to the seaside. This was a lovely and significant event which led to a continuing happy marriage of some 49 years at the time I write this.

After a while I was promoted within the Rolling Stock office to manage a small section dealing with garage staff matters and new engineering recruits, a not dissimilar task to that I was engaged on for operating staff in 1966.

In 1968, I applied for a post in the bus schedules office at 55 Broadway, which involved physically measuring new and changing road layouts enabling scheduled mileage to be calculated. This would involve working with a survey van within which there was a fifth wheel to be lowered when measuring sections of road needed. The head of Schedules was Norman Eagles and he was himself a transport enthusiast with a fantastic model railway which I was invited to see on one occasion. He ran an entire day's timetabled operations around this complex layout with a speeded-up clock.

Our small mileage section was actually based in Albany House, an annex to Broadway. Tony Wild ran the section which consisted of a lovely lady, Florrie, who mothered us both. Tony was also an enthusiast some 10 years older than I was. Usually on Tuesdays and Thursdays, we would take a couple of files with us to measure up certain sections of road, either for a new bus route, or perhaps because a one-way system was being introduced. Both Tony and I were avid photographers and since we still had the country area also under our remit, we would have some great days out measuring short sections of road in far flung parts of the empire, fitting in a great deal of photography on the way out and back. This was a new world of work

Photographed during one of the route measuring trips I made with Tony Wild in July 1969, RF 591 is in the middle of nowhere somewhere in Surrey.

for me which I found to be absolute bliss working with like-minded people. Tony and I remained friends and always meet up at one of the Brooklands events.

On one occasion out with the van, approaching Trafalgar Square to measure an altered section of road, I was pulled over by a policeman. A little shocked and not aware that I had committed any offence, I wound down the window, only to be questioned as to why I had run over a cyclist! A moment later it dawned that he had seen the fifth wheel and I was the butt of his joke.

When you love what you do, it is often the case that it is matched by good performance. It was not long before a post came vacant in the Statistical section of the schedules department and after being persuaded to move there initially at the same grade, I subsequently came to run that small section. By then, the Schedules Office had moved to palatial premises at 9/10 Grosvenor Place. This was 1971 and I had planned to marry the following year, so the extra earnings prevailed over my otherwise reluctance to leave the mileage section. I knew the work would not be to my taste, especially after working in the mileage section with its associated freedom and perks. The new job was routinely keeping statistical records of every schedule and its associated costs. The work came into its purpose when trade union negotiations were underway which might alter scheduling constraints, such as length of working day. The proposed scenario would then be costed and compared to existing conditions to work out extra staffing requirements and other effects on scheduling.

The other people on the section were all older women and we all looked after each other to cover perks we created. They often went for hair appointments during work time, and I used to travel far and wide to photograph the latest changes to the bus network during a 'long lunch', all in the days before flextime was officially heard of. Any queries as to absence were met with comments like 'oh she/ he went to lunch late today'. As it was, our boss Denis had previously managed the Stats section and was very tolerant and knowing of the way things ran. After Norman Eagles retired, his successors did not always appear to show his confidence and knowledge and would often call Denis and me in for long meetings with procrastination prevailing over possible changes to schedule conditions. Although these often dragged on well beyond normal finishing time, I admired the way Denis would suddenly just up and leave at 4.30 p.m., stating that he "had a train to catch", to the obvious dismay of our superiors. I was not then courageous enough to follow suit.

Years went by and despite applying unsuccessfully for a number of more interesting posts, I rekindled my desire to drive buses for a living. With Denis's help, I was moved into the care of Chiswick Training school in 1976. I had of course by then driven my own RTW since becoming 21 and thus had some idea of how to handle a bus. Nevertheless, there were certain bad habits that the Chiswick regime corrected during my training from which I maintained confidence driving around London. However, my serious weakness was (and still is!) reversing and many days of my training were spent in the yard trying not to knock over the skittles whilst driving backwards into a confined space. I was so relieved on the day of the examination to dispense with this agonising part of the test first during which I miraculously managed to reverse without knocking down the skittles. This left me full of confidence as I took RT 3800 through the gates of Chiswick works, although not through the well-practised hazards of central London, but a quiet gallop around very familiar Richmond town centre and back. That then was that. After 12 years with LT, followed then by type training on Routemasters, I had become a bus driver at Turnham Green, just 7 minutes' walk away from where we then lived at Acton Green.

Although I had become familiar with driving a bus full of people for some 7 years before this, it still felt somewhat daunting as I climbed into the cab of RM 159 on that first day as a service driver on route 27, firstly taking these unknowing passengers off towards Archway. I worked as a spare driver for a time working with a variety of conductors. After a while I was paired up with George who though a really nice person was not the best at his job. If we were to go anywhere something like on time, I had to constantly look into the bus to ensure the platform was clear and imagine my own double bell which George couldn't always remember to ring. Poor George really couldn't cope with a loaded bus and this came to a real head one day on the 117s.

Turnham Green was not a militant shed, and on occasions when nearby garages were involved in 'domestic' disputes, our Trade Union Rep, Rex would not agree to what often happened elsewhere in that a garage not directly involved in the dispute would cease to run their buses past the striking garage. We were junior partners on route 117 with only about 20% of its buses carrying our 'V' code. Hounslow (AV) was the major player of this then long route which at its fullest ran from Shepherds Bush to Staines and some even on to Egham. So, when Hounslow were in dispute, Turnham Green crews merely provided a skeleton service on the entire 117, enduring jeers from Hounslow pickets as we passed their garage. On one such occasion, travelling west and sweeping up loads of people at every stop, with a particularly 'duff' bus, ironically RM 117, I reached Syon Park and hearing no bell as usual, I turned around to see nothing other than a lower deck view blocked by so many people. I did note that the platform was clear, and so tried to move off, but the bus simply failed to gain purchase. Faced with this situation, I left the cab to look for George. After making my way upstairs through the throng, I saw him trapped up at the front trying to collect fares. I shouted my apologies to what must have been close to 100 people that the bus would no longer move due to the excessive loading and after eventually seeing the logic in this, somehow most of the excess load reluctantly left the vehicle.

After a time, I had a different conductor, a well-built man who had previously been in the police force in Glasgow. Once I had become tuned into his accent, I appreciated that he was someone who could read the telephone directory and make you laugh. His sense of humour was wry and immense. He also commanded the authority which poor George never could, so we never had any problems on the road with difficult people. I also got used to being rung away safely at every stop by this conductor. Archie was superb at his job, but had a pension for a tipple at regular intervals. The 27 was ideal for his purposes at Archway terminus, whereby Archie would dismount at the last stop along with the passengers and pop into the local hostelry whilst I took the bus round to the stand. When it came to departure time, I would take the bus around the gyratory system then in place and pick up passengers at the westbound stop in Junction Road along with a quenched Archie. The 117 had many short workings to Lower Feltham where the terminus was a two-stop bifurcation from the main route to Staines via Ashford Road. On those turns, Archie would jump off where there was a pub on the corner and I would carry on down to the terminus dropping people off on the way and doing my own bells. As with Archway, I would leave on time and pick up the waiting Archie on the corner just before turning right to rejoin Ashford Road. He was never not there on time.

The 117 was well timed and I do not remember needing a curtailment for late running. In fact it was too generously scheduled in the late evening and even at a gentle jog, it was necessary to leave Staines 15 to 20 minutes late if there was any chance of not being early by Hounslow. The 27 however could be very different and it was quite common for Camden Town to be the limit of an adjusted northbound trip to regain our southbound timing. There was a generous system then in place with 'dockets' which were effectively overtime payments which were handed in with other paperwork at the end of the shift. These were issued by a regulating inspector for late arrival both when finishing duty as one might expect, but also to my surprise even if you were late being relieved for your meal break. In both cases, up to 7 minutes late did not qualify, so naturally if a crew was only a few minutes late a couple of stops ahead of the relief point, they would always slow up slightly to make it 8 minutes. Then there was the 'double docket'. A minimum legal break was 40 minutes, but because of a wide range of scheduling complications, many shifts allowed more than this, with of course some 'spreadover' duties, effectively just covering the peak times, having a break of several hours. So long as there were more than 40 minutes break time, a late relieved crew could elect to take a 'double docket' and agree to take the second spell over on time, sacrificing part of their break. This 'double docket' would be as it says on this tin, double the delay time, so if the late relief was 10 minutes, to take a 'double docket' would result in a payment of 20 minutes overtime. It was beneficial to the continuity of the service for a crew to take a double docket so that they would be there to take their second bus on time, so it also became regarded as a 'favour' to the regulating

RM 583 with early body passes through Hounslow in August 1976 heading for what by then was the westernmost end of the route.

RT 3800 upon which I passed my PSV test in November 1976. Before it was a trainer, it swings round from Eden Street into Paradise Road, Richmond, a corner I later took her round on my test.

inspector to accept a 'double docket'. Additionally, there was another form of docket when an unscheduled bus movement was instructed to take a bus to and/or from the garage to the line of route prior to or after a staff cut. This also happened if a relieving crew were due to take over substantially late, although at Turnham Green, it was common for the empty bus to be left at the relief point. When I became a regulating inspector, I found that this was not usually the case elsewhere and thus more bus movement dockets were issued. All this sometimes meant in practice that the docket would be issued for much more than its actual time value if the second bus involved was a crucial journey, especially doctored to compensate any lost bus movement payment that could also be claimed and I confess to the guilt of issuing many well-enhanced dockets in my time, thus 'printing money', as a regulator later in my career to keep my service going.

Just a quick note about buses. It has always baffled me why identical machines produced by the same work force in the same factory perform so very differently from each other. I refer here to individual buses which I could discuss at great length, but RM 45 was worth a mention in its ability to go much faster than its sisters and to give a perfect and positive drive either in automatic or manual mode. Another very enjoyable and responsive bus to work from Turnham Green during my time was an experimental ex-Leeds Dennis

7517 UA, which was a test bed for the push button gears which became common on later vehicles such as Metrobuses. Drivers loved this machine which had marvellous acceleration, although conductors were never so keen since it lacked internal staunchions thus they had nothing but seatbacks to grab onto. The bus was restricted to route 27.

It was not long before I was sent for ticket training for one-person operation (OPO) and a standing secret that existed at V was carefully guarded by all OPO drivers. Once training had finished, one of the OPO drivers would warn of the 'cash problem' on route 91 without giving too much away. All you know was the phrase 'watch your cash on the Great West Road'. This riddle only unfolded on the first day operating the route around the Brentford area on the borough boundary between Ealing and Hounslow. Here existed a serious but not readily seen bump in the road surface and on day one, the unprepared new driver would find much of his cash catapulted out of the cash tray onto the floor. From that time onwards, the left arm was always at the ready at that point to cover the cash tray! This was not my only instance when a cash jackpot was hit. Whilst driving an E3 on one occasion clearly the flat fare box on an E3 had not been refitted properly after the previous day and a sudden drop with a deafening bang woke everyone up and the box split and showered the floor with coins by Turnham Green Station.

As I driver, whilst I never drank on duty, I am ashamed to confess to signing on for the first duty on route E3 at about 0515 hours whilst the effects of the previous night's 'session' were still frighteningly apparent on just one occasion back in about 1977. I shall never forget the extra concentration I had to apply on that first trip to Greenford that morning. It was a really terrible chance to have taken, but it taught me a valuable lesson and I have never since diced with alcohol anywhere near driving time.

Whilst the banter between driver and conductor was missed, there was nonetheless fun available on one-person operation. There were three daytime OPO routes from V during my stay there, all on a joint roster. The night route N97 was on a separate roster with volunteers, so thankfully I never had to work all night. Some parts of the E3 seemed to supply occasionally hostile passengers who would claim they had waited for hours for the bus. They were especially moaney before Metrobuses provided more room in 1981, but when I started we had SMSs on a route which desperately cried out for double-deckers. Nevertheless, although one or two of the early and late duties on this route were very short easy jobs. Not being a sports fan, I also often covered a Saturday turn for those seeking time to attend football games who were, in exchange, willing to give me an easy late or

early shift during the week. The late turns were also useful in paying maximum unsociable hours bonus and enabling me to spend time with my young children and also giving more time to spend photographing. The strangest event I encountered on the E3 was on return from Chiswick Pools one morning when a passenger alerted me to a passenger she thought was ill on the upper deck. I carried on to the next stop which was Turnham Green Church where I was also due for relief and the ambulance was called. They went upstairs by which time the person in question was declared not ill but dead. The bus was cleared of passengers and after giving a verbal statement I left the scene to my relieving colleague and the inspector.

Leyland Nationals replaced the SMSs but were miserable buses to work with and these came to be on the E3 before double-deckers finally took over. At night the interior lighting was always very dim. LSs also never felt very stable and in frosty, icy conditions, extra care was needed when descending Cuckoo Hill between Greenford and Hanwell. This was brought home to me late one night when on my last trip back to the garage, just after leaving the stop for Acton Town station on the short climb up to Acton itself. A Hanwell (HL) bus was going in the opposite direction and after a quick wave of the hand to each other, I heard this screech and looking in my mirror I could see that bus

An unusual design in London but a joy to drive - this Dennis was previously with Leeds.

was suddenly facing the same direction as me. He must have touched his brake too hard at the wrong moment on the icy road on the short descent which caused him to spin right round. Fortunately, all was otherwise OK and no collision occurred.

The E3 was also the route on which I had my only accident working for LT. It was entirely my fault, for roadworks at Hanwell where we turned off Uxbridge Road to go up towards Greenford were protected by a couple of heavy wooden baulks. On the first time I passed through this narrow channel very gingerly with no issue. Next time, I knew they were there and passed through the gap a little faster. The final occasion was disaster due to my over-confidence in that I caught the front door of the bus when I misjudged the width and brushed against the baulk. This caused the door to stick closed when I arrived at the next stop, so I continued to Greenford letting people enter via the middle doors. On checking the situation on the stand at Greenford, whilst there was very little sign of physical damage, I was unable to make the door mechanism function properly whatever I tried. There was no way out, I had to report the accident. Next day, I consulted Rex, our T.U.Rep on how I should handle this when called in to the manager, to which he replied –"Put it this way – what moved – the bus or the wooden baulk? – Just go in and apologise and sign up."

The 91 was a lovely route with each end having vastly different characteristics. The main challenge was to avoid the higgledy-piggledy pattern of the market stalls which encroached onto the road in North End Road, Fulham. At that end we passed through gentrified territory, whilst the western leg was a fast and often lonely (outside of factory start and finish times) run along the Great West Road. On late turns, I often went into 'automatic pilot' on this section, perhaps picking someone up at Gunnersbury and then nothing until returning to full consciousness to turn the steering wheel left into Hounslow West terminus. I once (the only occasion) got a tip from a very grateful poor drenched character on very stormy evening when I illegally paused between bus stops along this section to pick him up.

The 267 was our easiest route, with more than enough running time all day. A quiet poodle down to Hampton Court, often with long stand times there allowing perhaps 15 or 20 minutes sitting beside the river on a warm summer's afternoon made this a real delight. The only driving problem was a relatively tight turn from the stand on Hampton Court Station forecourt to achieve 180 degree turn back onto the very busy A309 to return towards Hammersmith. Stage one was to press the pedestrian crossing button which then caused the endless stream of traffic to halt by the time the cab had been regained. This gave passage onto the road into stationary traffic. This was usually a fine tuned

and successful operation, unless DMS1510 was the charge of the day. This bus, which somehow survived its contemporaries by many years, going on to become a training bus, had severely tight steering. On more than one occasion, I recall having to shunt back with embarrassment to finally make the right 180 degree turn by then holding up the impatient moving traffic.

The 267 was mainly a Fulwell route, but for them it always seemed as though they were struggling with their 'big day out' up town, compared to most of their other work which was mainly semi-rural. At a certain time in the afternoon, there were three rather boisterous school finishes to encounter along the way back to Hammersmith. Ahead of this, arrival at Hampton Court would find several FW buses parked up, many long due out before then. Their aim, I felt was to let the V bus go ahead and collect the school run, then go round us fast as possible empty to regain their time at Fulwell where the regulator would not suspect them to have left 'The Court' late. That was fine by me and I would go straight out a few minutes early and watch them all leap into their cabs behind me as I left. Yes, I got the first school, but that filled the bus leaving the two worse school mobs, for FW drivers to cater for, whereas I with a full load would often reach FW ahead of them, leaving them to face questions.

When in any industry dealing with the general public, there must always be some events which occur that are stranger than fiction. The buses were no exception, and route 267 was perhaps the scene of my strangest experience with any passenger. We were travelling east near Syon Park and I pulled into the stop before the canal. Two people boarded conventionally and I took the fares and issued tickets. During this transaction, a warning bell went off. This was not uncommon as children sometimes caused this by opening an emergency exit a little for a laugh. Since the bus was stationary, I finished the transaction and then as I was about to leave my seat to clear the problem, then amid enormous hails of laughter from the back of the bus. At the same time, I heard a 'tap tap' on my offside window. I regained my seat and slid open the window to be greeted by a rather posh female voice asking "How does one get into this bus?" It transpired that she had attempted to get in from the middle of the road via the rear off-side emergency door.

Late turns on the E3 were particularly easy, none moreso than one Boxing Day when a performing 'straight' shift (i.e. no break) of less than 4 hours during which I carried nobody at all, and earned an enormous bonus plus two days off in lieu. Almost equally unproductive was one winter Sunday evening when I was rostered to cover the penultimate E3, but due to a crew driver calling in sick, I was contacted earlier in the day and asked to cover duty 14 on route 27 instead. This was the last 27 and was a short 'straight' shift which

LS 238 is about to pass under the 14'6" bridge in Acton Lane, alleged to be the reason that DMSs could not be used on the route, although the type did so when as training buses.

did not sign on till almost 2000 hours and finished about 0030. It was scheduled as Teddington-Archway-Teddington and finish. All was fine when we took the bus over, but by the time we got to Teddington, the snow had fallen thick and fast. After a long scheduled stand time, we prepared to leave for Archway, but the wheels just spun and spun. An Inspector also tried to move our bus but with the same negative result. Eventually an engineer arrived with a beach full of sand, but this was very much later and we were now on time for just our last Teddington to Turnham Green trip.

I thoroughly enjoyed a lovely time driving buses although one day in 1978 a local ticket inspector suggested that I should consider applying for a promotion to his grade on the grounds that, whilst youth and health might be on your side for now, nobody knows what might be around the corner. It did get me thinking and I was ready for a change by then. I applied and was accepted but as a regulator rather than a ticket inspector. That and my many years with London Transport and its successors is a story for another time.

DMS 1504 arrives at Syon Lane on a curtailed late running 91 westbound journey. Many passengers queried the location of this parochial destination, once more clearly defined as 'Osterley Syon Lane' on earlier blind sets. A much more familiar name for this location was and is Gillette Corner.

AROUND THE TOWN FOR HALF A CROWN
Leon Daniels OBE

It was the Festival of Britain that prompted London Transport to introduce a circular tour of London (Service J) in 1951.

A small group of RTs, including currently preserved and overseas tour veteran RT 1702, and fitted with public address systems ran what would today be called a 'walk-up' service for a two hour trip around the capital. The fare was 2/6 and the title of this chapter reflects how it was initially marketed. It then returned each year and by 1962 RMs had replaced RTs. Sadly, the endemic staff shortages made it impossible to continue with double-decker buses and hired-in coaches were introduced after the 1963 season, running, as ever from Victoria, Buckingham Palace Road.

By 1972 London Transport, feeling a touch of radical marketing, wanted to reintroduce double-deckers. As well as new DMSs, amazingly arrived a sprinkling of hired elderly East Kent Guy Arab open-top vehicles which were instantly popular. The success spurred London Transport on further and thanks to a close friendship between publisher & vintage vehicle enthusiast Prince Marshall and Roy Smith at London Transport a fleet of seven Midland Red D9s arrived for the 1975 season. Converted to open top by LPC Coachworks at Hounslow, and based and crewed from Stockwell garage, they commenced their long London second life.

The story now diverges. Hired coaches were marginalised, although firms like Maybury of Cranbourne continued to participate, and there were more double deckers – internally supplied DMSs plus also some convertible roof Daimler Fleetlines acquired from Bournemouth Transport. The London Transport Round London Sightseeing Tour was hampered by bureaucratic inefficiency and high costs. Despite being an almost monopoly provider of such services the negativity of London Transport was impossible to suppress. I was once told by the Senior Inspector at Piccadilly Circus not to send him open toppers because the queue got too long and was impossible to manage... another story for another book.

From 1978 Prince Marshall's Obsolete Fleet was contracted to provide its D9 fleet with its own staff. They ran from rented premises which happened to be the old Nunhead Garage subsequently used by Banfield Coaches and its successors. I joined at this point in the story as a part-time driver and then more.

The original operation was operated by RTs until 1962 as shown in these two photos from the London Transport Magazine.

DMS 1256 was the first of its class to be sold for further service – to Ted Brakell from Ensignbus which was taking all redundant DMSs from London Transport. It immediately went into service with Obsolete Fleet running five two-hour tours per day from Nunhead Garage. I collected it from Richmond and delivered it myself. There was an immediate negative response from LT staff concerning how vehicles were being sold and then used to by private contractors on their own services. Nevertheless it represented a great step forward in terms of comfort for both passengers and drivers and was the first of a significant number of DMSs to be used on sightseeing tours. Just about all DMSs prepared for further service by Ensignbus were converted to semi-automatic gearchange and despite sightseeing buses operating in the heart of London's difficult traffic conditions reliability was very high.

I well remember my first day sightseeing, with OM 3. No type training, no route learning. I was sent to Marble Arch with a map. The tour in those days was able to cover much ground in two hours – west to Kensington and Royal Albert Hall and east as far as Tower Bridge with four river crossings. The D9 was built for Midland Red in the same way that the Routemaster was built for London. They share some similarities including chassisless construction, hydraulic brakes and power steering. A key difference was that the typical stops-per-mile were fewer in the Birmingham market so a key Routemaster feature – accumulators to store energy – was not fitted. On the D9 therefore you only had power assistance in proportion to your road speed. So after a decent run at 30mph or so the brakes were nicely powerful to achieve a stop. However in slow-moving London traffic the brake pedal could become very hard and you needed all your strength to halt the bus. Much the same applied to the steering and midway into a turn the steering could become very hard. (On Routemasters you 'borrow' from the accumulators the power you need). As a result the D9 came with a really powerful handbrake and on most days there were always occasions when you grabbed it on the move to aid your stopping, as well as selecting neutral to disconnect the engine. More than once I yanked the handbrake so far I banged the window behind me with my elbow. Fortunately most sightseeing passengers were upstairs……

A D9's brakes came with one further complication. Interestingly the brake cylinders were not mounted in the wheels but on the frame which supported them. We fund that the all important seals fitted to them reacted very badly to certain types of brake fluid (which – by definition – must be non-compressible material). They would swell up, pop out of position and you would now be leaking brake fluid. The result for the driver was something very often experienced in BMC cars of the period – the first press of the brake pedal alarmingly did almost nothing and you had to pump them a couple of times to get some pressure. That was not too bad if you were planning a smooth stop but terrifying if you needed to 'jump' on the brakes because of some other inconsiderate motorist. In particular it is very counter-intuitive to a human bus driver who wants more brake effort to release the brake pedal rather than press down even harder!

Obsolete Fleet also ran an OM on route 74Z between Baker Street and The Zoo, and from March 1980 vintage ST922 resumed on route 100 between Oxford Circus and the newly opened London Transport Museum at Covent Garden. I worked on those too. ST 922 remains a beautiful bus to drive. Indeed I passed my 'manual' PSV licence on it at the long-gone test centre on Balls Pond Road. It is light and its petrol engine gives a sparkling performance. Petrol engines, however, run very hot. In the winter this – the only heater – is most welcome but in the summer quite the reverse. Of course it has a crash

This remarkable photograph was taken at the second Obsolete Fleet Nunhead Garage. It had vacated the front section still owned by London Transport in about 1981 and moved to a long-since sold part of the original garage at the rear. One surviving maintenance pit was re-excavated and a paint shop installed. Captured here are both former Devon General Regent Vs (the extreme rear of 507 RUO, the only one to be painted red is at far left). Along with ST 922, one of the D9s bought and used with a covered top, an open top D9 on the pit, and finally RT 1 far right.

In 1977 the 25 Silver Jubilee Routemasters were lined up in Hyde Park forming a procession to Battersea Park. OM 4 led the cavalcade with a jazz band, followed by RT 1599, both having been especially prepared. The Obsolete Fleet vehicles were always in demand for special occasions and it became a source of irritation to the Livingstone regime at the GLC from 1981 that only the private sector could provide vehicles for such events. One particular embarrassment was Transport Committee Chair Dave Wetzel having to drive an OM in the 'Fares Fair' campaign.

Two AEC Regent Vs joined Obsolete Fleet in 1979. Originally they were intended to arrive in time to work on the Christmas Lights service 7L the previous year but did not arrive in time. They were acquired to operate the second season of route 74Z (Baker Street-The Zoo) as one-man operated vehicles, replacing the single crew operated OM the previous season. In the event they only materialised part way through the season. Driver fare collection was achieved through the narrow window to the driver's nearside. DRO 1 was the only one of the pair to be repainted in red livery.

gearbox which requires accurate double declutching both going up and down the box. The very last part of the travel is a 'clutch stop' which stops the rotation of the transmission input shaft. You need it to select a starting gear, it helps deliver a crunch-free upshift provided you only use it on the second depressing of the clutch from neutral to a higher gear, and you don't want to use it at all changing down. And if your left hand didn't have anything else to do there are a pair of levers on the side of the engine compartment wall. One is a hand throttle – you would typically use it when cold to keep the minimum engine speed up. The other controls the advance and retarding of the delivery of the spark

from the distributor to each cylinder's spark plugs. This affects the power produced by each cylinder on each stroke which in itself changes depending on what you are asking the engine to do – speeding up, pulling on load, or overrunning with no load. So the position of the advance and retard lever will be critical to avoid engine damage and deliver most power at numerous stages of any bus journey.

For many of the 'Nunhead' years the regular ST driver was the irascible Frank Peacock who was as typical cockney as you might get. He had fruity language and frequently told other motorists what he thought of them through the open offside cab. He was

Route 100 returned in yet another guise in 1980 when it operated from the newly opened London Transport Museum at Covent Garden to Oxford Circus (and later to Marble Arch). ST 922 was the normal vehicle used but on suitable days the 1925 Dennis D 142 was used. This era was one where people could travel on these unique vehicles at ordinary fares. Nowadays such opportunities would be targeted at an audience with greater spending power. Operating a bus in London's traffic with two-wheel brakes, a crash gearbox and no protection for the driver was always a challenge yet this vehicle performed admirably and remains in preservation.

also incredibly proud of being in charge of a unique vehicle on London's roads. His wife often would act as a conductor although for most of the time the ST was conducted by the legendary Harry Cook. A former Croydon Corporation tram driver he used the small print of the terms of its sale to the London Passenger Transport Board to continue to be a bus driver long past his formal retirement age. When the GLC made London Transport introduce new 'friendly' minibuses in 1972 Harry was a natural choice for selection to join the P4 rota given his eternally sunny disposition and knowledge. There was, however, a point in his 70s when he had to retire and so joined Obsolete Fleet as the completely authentic vintage bus conductor.

He also opened up the garage, put oil and water in the buses, reconciled and paid in the takings, saw the buses in at night and locked up.

A pause for a lovely interlude. Route 74Z (which replaced a supplementary schedule on route 74) took six minutes during which time the conductor had to collect up to 72 fares. We had a minute to go around the block at The Zoo and also at Baker Street. Every few trips we ran to Allsop Place for a tea break and once a day for lunch. Roughly 40 single trips a day.

It was so popular we were asked to double the frequency and use two buses (We bought two Devon General AEC Regent Vs 507 and 508 RUO suitable for single-person operation but they weren't quite ready....). So for a few days we used two OMs but with one conductor. The venerable Harry Cook would collect all the fares on stand at Baker Street with bus 1 and send it off. Then he would board bus 2 and collect the fares, before alighting half way, crossing the road, and catching bus number 1 again on its return journey and collecting any fares there. After lunch he did the same thing but worked from The Zoo end instead. The only case ever in London of two buses being conducted all day by one conductor?

When the winter came London Transport devised a night-time open top bus route to see the Christmas Lights. It started at 7L from Marble Arch to Tottenham Court Road. In due course it became 12L and ran to Trafalgar Square instead. London Transport provided conductors from Victoria Garage. Somehow I became the schedules manager and team captain for the Christmas Lights service and in 1979 I joined Obsolete Fleet full time as Manager.

Underpinning Obsolete Fleet's business was a lucrative advertising contract. Johnnie Walker had sponsored the restoration and operation of ST 922 and they too expanded into the London sightseeing market. It should be clear that the value of 'opportunities to see' (advertising-speak) of an open top bus only in the West End and City was much more valuable than the advertising on a bus running between South Croydon and Shepherds Bush.

In due course Obsolete Fleet became a fairly sizeable business. Besides running services for London Transport (years before bus route tendering had ever been thought of) on sightseeing tours, 74Z, 100 and then alternative tours like 'Back Street London' from Baker Street Station, it was doing restorations, painting, promotional work and film/tv assignments. And somehow at the height of the summer season we decamped to Crich Transport Museum to manage and operate the annual Transport Extravaganza as well.

Our fleet of D9s was supplemented by the two AEC Regent Vs and our daily operations supported by long-term hires from the preservationist/entrepreneur Ted Brakell, whose Northern General Routemasters were on continuous hire to us one way or another.

In 1980 excursions and tours were deregulated and from that time it was possible to get a licence to run sightseeing buses in London almost without limitation, thanks to the defective legislation. London Transport's only competitor had been Cityrama which ran tours in multiple languages. Other companies then arrived on the scene – Ebdon's Tours, London Crusader, London Sightseeing Tours (a rival faction from inside the Maybury family) and others. Embarrassingly for the giant London Transport, they all used former DMSs sold by the authority and which now came back to compete with them.

Then one day the sky fell in on us. Prince Marshall was not a well man. He was indeed the UK's longest surviving sickle-cell anaemia patient. The many years of regular blood transfusions and other effects caused his kidneys to fail and he ended up on dialysis as well.

One day in 1981, when I was at the by-now-closed Stonebridge Garage working with some buses on a film starring Michael York called "Success is the Best Revenge." We had a complicated bus sequence to do. I got an urgent message from Prince. Out of the blue there was a donor kidney for him and a transplant was possible imminently. Somehow as soon as we wrapped the filming I visited him in hospital armed – not realising the consequences – with his draft will to be signed.

We will fast-forward. Prince never left St Mary's Hospital, Paddington and a catalogue of medical problems, bad luck and negligence ended his life. We were with him at the end. On the night of his death our close friend Tim Nicholson – the architect of ST 922's restoration – and I took over the last journey on route 100 from Covent Garden and were a crew to Oxford Circus and back. It was the only way to deal with our grief.

Obsolete Fleet was a sole proprietorship and his last will placed his vintage vehicle assets into a perpetual trust (which is not really legal). So was set a scene which doomed Obsolete Fleet to failure, which occurred in 1983.

London Pride Sightseeing's business model relied on the extensive sale of all-over advertisement contracts. For most of this period London Transport did not sell such a product. One of the most unusual ones was DMS 586 which advertised Castlemaine XXXX beer. This ex-Ebdons vehicle not only was it 'roughed up' to look dirty and battered, but it was fitted with a 'kangaroo bar' (also deliberately bent) and a sheep's head! It finished its days at Chicago Motor Coach Company.

As sightseeing traffic grew National Bus Company became Involved in two ways. London Country became a contractor to London Transport providing Atlanteans whilst the new enterprise London Crusader entered the market in their own right using four Atlanteans including AN II here. In general the public sector operators suffered from the effects of a lack of enthusiasm from many of the staff. Drivers and departure supervisors hoped for insufficient support for the last trip of the day so giving an early finish. At London Pride and others we were pushing to run more and more trips. London Crusader's reign in London was therefore short. They ran 1983-5. For 1986 it transformed into the Green Line sightseeing tour but that was the last appearance.

So, when I woke up to a life without Prince or Obsolete Fleet I worked out that there was a business in running sightseeing tours supported by commercial advertising. The drain on Obsolete Fleet had been the vintage vehicle restoration as well as trying to service the estate and consequences of the will, which had turned out to be badly drafted. Peter Newman at Ensignbus thought likewise. So, with Peter's huge support we launched London Pride Sightseeing.

One day whilst in 55 Broadway I had spotted an interesting plan for the dispersal of the sightseeing buses from the lucrative Eros Island stop at Piccadilly Circus, which was due to close permanently. Coventry Street was one of them and when I looked at it, it was magic. No through traffic, huge pedestrian footfall from Leicester Square and the redevelopment of the Trocadero site, soon to open. That's where we would go. My competitors laughed at me. Eros Island was pure gold. You were guaranteed a full load as soon as you got to the front of the queue. You just waited behind Cityrama, Ebdons, LT etc. Over in Coventry Street it was quiet. We had our back to Piccadilly Circus and the Trocadero was a building site. But we launched.

Actually it was a false start. 1st April 1984. Our buses weren't ready but Peter Newman had secured a cheap hire of one of the luxury Van Hool Astromegas used by Southend Transport on route X1 to London which were idle during the day. We would get three trips out of it Monday to Friday. First tour and we got four passengers

– not bad from nothing. £10 in revenue on day 1 trip 1. We celebrated. I bought the crew hamburgers from a nearby outlet.

But the Astromega would not start. Dead as a dodo. We had to give the passengers their money back. In fact we had to use our own money as we had used their £10 to buy hamburgers. Eventually – mid afternoon – a Metrobus from Westbourne Park garage eventually arrived to be a jump start. It then picked up its Southend-bound passengers and went home.

Peter Newman counselled me not to be downhearted. That was difficult. We actually had negative revenue on the first day. It got better after that. We had decent loads on the weekday Astromega and at weekends we had our first bus DMS 648. It was only partially painted. In fact each weekend it came back with a bit more on it. Eventually it was white, purple and orange diagonal stripes – Peter's choices which matured over time into a really nice colour scheme.

Ensignbus was making open-top DMSs as fast as they could for all the operators. We soon had ours and then came that magic moment in business. Eros Island was closed as part of the long-planned road scheme and the hosted operators banished. Ebdons to Regent Street, London Transport to Haymarket etc. That golden goose of Eros Island was no more AND the Trocadero opened in Coventry Street and suddenly half of London was walking past us.

But the business plan relied on advertising revenue

London Pride took a batch of former three-axle Metroliner National Express coaches and made them into open-top. Up to 65 seats could be achieved on the upper deck. These were outstanding vehicles especially on busy summer days. At this time two of the more traditional 'upper class' tour operators, Evan Evans and Frames Rickards who were famed for their expensive, escorted coach tours, also wanted to join the revolutionary 'turn up and go' product. They both made deals with existing operators in return for one vehicle to operate in their livery. Frames Rickards chose the ill-fated and short lived London Tour Company which lasted only part of one season, and Even Evans ran for several years with London Pride.

The progressive consolidation of sightseeing operations brought a variety of vehicles into the London Pride fleet. 264 was a Leyland Olympian owned by Cityrama which had been converted into a part open top configuration. These vehicles had an even longer season span of operation since there were enough covered seats for even the worst days. By now London Pride had replaced all advertising liveries with this red and silver scheme and was selling a 24-hour ticket (pioneered unsuccessfully by Culture Bus) with more routes to spread the journey possibilities and passengers over a wider area. This service ran out to Docklands and Greenwich giving passengers a ride on the Woolwich Ferry.

and we were spectacularly successful. There were no 'overall advertising' buses in those days. Our fleet was confined to the lucrative West End and City and we lapped up blue-chip advertising clients – Burger King, Marks and Spencer, Beefeater Gin, 7UP, Tetley Tea. So many it was hard to find a fleet-liveried bus in service.

In 1986 with its ever decreasing market share and high costs, London Transport fought back using Routemasters. It finally found an adjective that the competitors couldn't use – it became 'The ORIGINAL London Transport Sightseeing Tour' (we had all adopted 'Official' when they started using it). The Routemaster phase meant the end of all hired-in operations and since Ensignbus was no longer a contractor Peter Newman took a much greater interest in London Pride Sightseeing, not forgetting the fact that he and his family had all been managing departures and selling tickets on summer weekends for it for some time!

Over time we absorbed some of the other operators. Many had found the loss of Eros Island ('a licence to print money') very difficult. There were huge complaints from the frontagers by the displaced locations which caused friction with Westminster City Council and the 'walk up trade' was reduced. Market consolidation was needed and we took in Ebdons, Cityrama and several others.

Back in Coventry Street we were happy. In fact business grew throughout the day so much that we were running sightseeing tours well into the evening and eventually the night. Tours at midnight were not known. During the pre-Christmas period we reinvented the old 7L and ran Coventry Street to Marble Arch with open toppers. We had full loads most nights and the only headwind was the very slow traffic which meant our buses only came back slowly.

The original Round London Sightseeing Tour gave passengers a map. In time the competition forced improvements and some operators provided live guides. London Transport had to use the terribly expensive and posh Blue Badge Guides but most operators let the drivers or unqualified guides do it.

So did we – London Pride had separate guides, working from a script but free to make their own personal version of it. The guide team were great but they did double the staff cost of every trip. Moreover their individual personalities did produce an inconsistent result. They also got tired, had bad days, and were saying broadly the same thing three or four times a day so the quality often deteriorated towards the end of it.

So one day I started experimenting with audio cassette tapes. With the help of some Ensignbus electrical experts we rigged an auto-reverse cassette player in DMS 648 and connected it to a pause footswitch in the cab. I made, from memory really, a commentary using a domestic cassette machine and we took it out on route. It played out through the bus speakers well enough and all the driver needed to do was press the footswitch to suit the conditions.

Then I got more ambitious and added music, sound effects (like Big Ben chiming no matter what the time was) and other features. These turned out to be very popular. Of course it was not as good as a great guide but it was consistent, there were no complaints about inaccuracies and it never got tired and called in sick. We went over to 100% audio cassette and a small studio was built at Purfleet (in one end of my Portakabin!) which had enough equipment and soundproofing to make a great job.

The production really got under way. There were tapes for daytime and night-time (there are things you can see at night but not during the day – and vice versa), and we had versions for bridge closures, special events and so on. I was voicing all of the tapes which was a big workload but I was superbly assisted by my Operations Manager John Burch who was (and still is) a Radio Caroline supporter and knew lots about audio recording. We were locked away in our studio for hours.

Later we branched out into multi-language tours using some really clever 8-track cassette equipment which was well ahead of anything anyone else was using and of course now it is all digital. Sadly is no longer my voice but I have a good selection of old tapes.

These were undoubtedly the heyday of sightseeing tours and under Peter Newman's direction London Pride Sightseeing gradually took out the competition. First to go was Culture Bus. Set up by two Australian women the yellow DMSs ran what we would now call a 'Hop-on Hop-off' tour. We bought it out of the failing Trathens business. The takeover was rather dramatic. I went to the receivers in Puddle Dock with a bankers draft. That evening the Culture Bus staff and vehicles had congregated for a wake in a pub in south west London. A team of us went to collect the vehicles – there was no way the inebriated staff were going to drive them anyway. We all went for a vehicle each – in my case the single Metropolitan double decker and former London Transport MD 6. Of course as soon as the engines were started the noise was noticed by the now rather animated Culture Bus staff and a lynching mob emerged from the pub. "They're stealing our buses!" was the cry.

Well of course the DMSs built up their air quite quickly and were on their way but my Metropolitan was still working on its air suspension, doors, air throttle and gears. Now there was only me and my lynching mob was coming up the side of MD 6. I already had the drive selected and the handbrake off. Moments before they were aboard her air suspension jumped up, the doors slammed shut and in true Metropolitan fashion we shot away like a scalded cat and to safety.

The following day we ran a full Culture Bus service despite some vehicle shortcomings and the late Derek Giles, the Operations Director at Southend Transport personally directed operations from our office at 60 St James's Street. During the quiet winter we could run it inside London Pride Sightseeing and save costs. In the summer it ran independently.

Culture Bus was rather ahead of its time. Today all the sightseeing tours offer the 'hop on and hop off' service with tickets valid for 24 hours. But they didn't quite catch the market. In our case we sold Culture Bus to Southend Transport as a way for them to occupy the large number of vehicles laying over idle in the middle of the day between commuter journeys but sadly the venture ended as that company withdrew increasingly from the whole Southend-London market as the parallel rail service dramatically improved.

At Peter Newman's instigation there was a concerted effort to grow the sightseeing business. The sale of advertising space was wound down in favour of the London Pride Sightseeing brand. Former National Express tri-axle Metroliners were added, capable of multi-language commentaries and could carry 65 fare-payers on the upper deck. The 'hop on and off' concept was considerably enhanced and the 24 hour ticket allowed interchange with overlapping services serving other attractions including westward to South Kensington and eastwards beyond Tower Hill.

The 24-hour ticket was further enhanced when interchange was introduced with City Cruises' river services. Indeed, some of their fleet were adorned as 'This is an official London Sightseeing Boat' signage. The rationale was clear. People were attracted to the 24-hour ticket but few used it intensively. Having bought a ticket mid-morning, by the time they had taken a decent ride and stopped for lunch, there was only a bit of time before the day was over. And every fare-paying passenger that was at lunch, in a tourist attraction or on a boat meant a bus seat that could be resold to another passenger. In time tourist attraction entry tickets, phone cards and other revenue-generative lines were added. Revenue was now very strong.

Another innovative scheme – also pioneered by Peter Newman – was the way in which we dealt with cash. In those days credit and debit card transactions were quite low although we did take them. The vast majority of sales were cash and that left a lot of cash on the street – open to theft. Our team was stuck with a security risk and an expensive bank night safe operation.

We struck a deal with a Bureau de Change chain named 'Chequepoint' which was open long hours every day across London. Staff deposited cash with them and within a couple of days they sent us the money by

Another 'luxury' brand that tried the London Sightseeing market was Harrods. Two Neoplan N122 double deckers ran from the Knightsbridge store operated by Eurocare Ltd in the early 1980s. There have been sporadic operations since and in 2000 Arriva (the operator of the Original London Sightseeing Tour) used RM 1919 in Harrods livery and with luxury seats.

bank transfer. This was a real win-win. They needed sterling to sell to tourists and we were providing it. We needed to get our cash off the street and they took it. Over the period of operation tens of million pounds were transacted and both parties delighted with the arrangement.

In December 1990 the local bus service business of Ensignbus was told to CNT Holdings – the same parent that owned Citybus Hong Kong – and I went with it. That mostly ended my formal association with the management of sightseeing buses in London although for a long period afterwards I still scripted and voiced the recorded commentaries. When Ensignbus sold London Pride Sightseeing to a consortium in 1998 this continued for a short while but the new owners failed to succeed with the business. London Pride was eventually absorbed by Arriva as The Original Tour having been bought back by Ensignbus for a short period in 2000/01.

Thus – in my view – ended the heyday of sightseeing bus operation in London. From a modest start in 1951 millions of passengers enjoyed an upper deck ride around London on an ever-developing product. Today the market is mostly shared by two operators The Original Tour is the direct descendent of the London Transport Round London Sightseeing Tour and is owned by RATPDev. The other is Big Bus Tours which can trace its roots back a part of the Maybury family from Cranbourne which was a sub-contracted coach company to London Transport all those years ago. It now operates in many cities around the world.

The advent of the internet has significantly changed the market, whilst it is now very much more difficult to get boarding points and stands approved. Environmental restrictions also now mean that using cheap second-hand buses is no longer acceptable and they need to be new.

The companies now operate under much more regulated conditions than we did. As a result the commercial flair has disappeared from the street and is now housed at Head Office. No longer do we hear the words "who wants to do another trip?" on the pavement beside a tour bus which was due to finish but where people were asking for more!

4 STORIES OF A MANAGEMENT TRAINEE
Michael Walton

I started work with London Transport in October 1972, perhaps surprisingly as a Graduate Trainee given that I hadn't been to University. With the arrogance of a very clever 19 year old (which wasn't an opinion shared by anyone else), I fully expected London Transport to be particularly welcoming and keenly awaiting my reforming talents. I was to be by varying degrees rather disappointed at the lack of enthusiasm for my exceptional gifts.

The first posting was to Recruitment in Griffith House, the nondescript office block in Old Marylebone Road. I was assigned to an elderly curmudgeonly interviewer and assessor who immediately ordered me to to get a 'proper' haircut (thereby removing my then fashionable long blond locks). In the two weeks of misery endured I learned that London Transport (in his mind) had no interest whatsoever in women, ethnic minorities or indeed any other minority group joining

the august organisation, and their recruitment was a matter of considerable regret made necessary by the lack of 'suitable' applicants. I never again encountered such overt racism in my career and I departed with considerable relief.

District and Piccadilly lines staff office at Earl's Court was my next assignment and was an altogether better experience. Something of a gulf existed between staff and traffic functions which I couldn't work out if it was animosity or rivalry, but the rather old fashioned team worked remarkably well and achieved innumerable small but collectively great things to keep the lines operating.

Other postings followed, most notably within the Chief Mechanical Engineer's huge Chiswick Works complex. One particularly dull task was working in the Engineer's Bonus Section, along with dozens of predominantly female staff (often partners or

For almost all of the 1970s, RTs and DMSs were operated simultaneously by London Transport and could often be seen together. The RT's life had been extended by poor bus purchasing decisions in the late 1960s and LT's disastrous interference with manufacturers' engineering specs.

relatives of male operating staff), ploughing through endless reams of paperwork calculating weekly bonus payments for bus mechanics and garage staff undertaking their standard duties. It was immediately apparent that a fixed wage incorporating an average of bonus payments would dispense with the large clerical staff and improve garage efficiency by negating the need to generate so much paperwork.

Another spell inside the works and a bus garage, studying huge inventories of newly manufactured or overhauled bus components, left me wondering why only London Transport bothered with such costly activities. The purchase of large numbers of single deck AEC Merlins and Swifts was clearly disastrous and to follow this, throughout the 1970s, London Transport purchased a huge fleet of Daimler Fleetlines but seemed to care little for them. The only vehicle that seemed to matter to Chiswick's engineers was the Routemaster, undeniably brilliant (after many years of expensive development) for the 1950s and 1960s but economically largely redundant for the very different world of the 1970s and 1980s.

Charles Greystock, the affable Chief Mechanical Engineer, asked me at the end of my time at Chiswick to summarise my experiences. I regaled the foregoing conclusions with the relish of an enthusiastic trainee keen to be recognised as a singular visionary. After some moments of thought, Mr Greystock stood and looked out of his office window and surmised 'I can't disagree with much you have said but you understand nothing about politics'. I didn't have the nerve to ask him why the Daimler Fleetline was so disliked by London Transport. Because of the posting I also began to understand the power wielded by some Trade Unions who by differing degrees both helped and hindered their members. London Transport was never minded to confront the unions and always remained wary of their power whatever the issue. I left his office chastened but wiser about how complicated (and conservative) London Transport's organisation really was and doubting the wisdom of volunteering challenging observations.

An interesting assignment was to Fares and Charges at 55 Broadway, one posting to the Scholar's section and another to Season Tickets. Both sections were well run and productive. A team were involved in working out 'on demand' season ticket rates and special fares from Underground to British Rail stations and particularly in the case of suburban London traffic this seemed odd. A simple zonal fares formula would have saved much time and effort and of course staff resource. Such suggestions caused mirth, not because the team were resistant to the idea, but that there was no political will for change and the interests of passengers were surprisingly deemed unimportant by senior management. Life carried on as usual.

Still at 55 Broadway, Public Relations (where I learned how to write succinctly) and then to Publicity (again at Griffith House) to a 'proper' job. Both departments were under the wing of the Chief Public Relations Officer (the avuncular and gentlemanly F.E. Wilkins), but operated very differently. Public Relations largely dealt with the huge volume of mail and telephone calls, nearly always complaints about deteriorating standards of bus and tube services and was commensurately dispiriting after unremitting abuse received on the phone. Considerable backlogs of correspondence amassed in my time there although no extra resource was ever forthcoming. The department felt resigned to perpetual misery and seemed to singularly fail to be proactive in any positive way. Occasionally I was called upon to attend (and report back on) public meetings discussing public transport issues and on one occasion in Sutton was harangued by the audience when I was introduced as a 'London Transport observer'. The large audience were furious with bus services that either didn't run or were running in convoys. Added to the then Northern line woes which were infuriating Morden commuters, the clear impression to the local population was that London Transport was failing in its duty to manage its portfolio properly. This somewhat threatening experience was reported back without reaction.

At the time I lived for a while in Streatham and, like many other young Londoners, I eagerly awaited Saturday nights to go to town and squander all that remained of my meagre salary. I worked out that the latest way I could get home was on the last Victoria line train to Brixton and whether by accident or design there was a 109 bus from Kennington to Streatham which 'connected'. Seeing the hoards who swarmed the aged RT type bus came initially as a shock. If the conductor was benign then all available space up, down and in between was jammed. If not, then five standing was the limit and gaggles of weary travellers would stagger up Brixton Hill. Study of the elusive Night Bus timetable revealed that most Night Bus routes had no Saturday night/Sunday morning service at all and service patterns were intended for night workers who had long since resorted to driving to and from work or (in the case of the Docks) industry had closed down. Here was an obvious market completely ignored by London Transport. The Staff Suggestion scheme was much publicised internally and I wrote what I considered an intelligent case for meaningful Saturday night buses and in due course received a starchy and negative reply. I persevered and again in due course was called in to be sternly told that I wasn't to meddle in a business I knew nothing about.

A few years later (and now living in Chiswick) with the opening of the Piccadilly line extension to Heathrow a 30 minute, all night, every night N97 was introduced from Trafalgar Square to Heathrow. At weekends it was mobbed in Trafalgar Square and the intention of carrying passengers to Heathrow was proven irrelevant but clubbers travelling back to suburban homes crammed the wonderfully speedy Metrobuses. A new world was born and in due course a decent Night Bus network was operational throughout London. The N97, as an example, was much increased in weekend frequency as far as Brentford to cater for the enormous traffic demands. The rest is history but after so many wasted, miserable and entirely inactive years, London Transport was forced to confront the inevitable shift in what its customers wanted.

Publicity (apart from its hidden shop) had little to do with the public directly but nearly every aspect of its work had a direct or indirect visual output. From temporary and permanent signage, timetable, leaflet, book, map and poster design, production and distribution, photography and film and more, a largely cohesive department did what it had to do, sometimes wonderfully and sometimes woefully. It was quickly apparent that some staff had complete freedom to do exactly as they pleased and others were in regimented positions. As was common in many other departments, a signing-in book within sight of the Staff Clerk was rigidly policed. In Publicity's case the start time was 08.30 with a red line being drawn at 08.35 and anyone later than this was subject (after a few transgressions) to disciplinary action. This might have been acceptable but for some office staff this didn't seem to apply. They came and went as they pleased and in some sections afternoon attendance after a lengthy lunch in a local pub seemed voluntary. Nothing was ever said. I worked in various 'regimented' sections (Road, Rail and Shop) where my burgeoning interest in posters, their design and their influence was encouraged. I owe a debt of gratitude to Howard Butler and Chris Godbold, both great managers, and Road and Rail Inspectors, Peter Baldwin, Eddie Payne and Alf Sharman. They all taught me in different ways so much about how to be an effective professional employee and each was very much focused on delivering the best possible service to the public. As for some other Publicity staff, their barely accountable but charmed lives carried on as ever. Another anomaly of London Transport life was its regularly updated Staff Manual which within its

In 1979, the year before the LT Museum opened, London Transport made a considerable effort to commemorate the 150 years of buses in London since George Shillibeer began his horse omnibus service. This large rally was held at Battersea Park and in the distance can be seen buses in a special 'Shillibeer' livery.

massive loose bound form laid out the intricate detail of what was expected of an employee. Every section ended with the caveat 'Subject to the discretion of the Employing Officer'. It had become clear from my experience that each department operated to its own interpretation of the rule book, which perhaps in the case of Publicity was an 'a la carte' selection of what suited.

Basil Hooper (formerly with British Transport Hotels) was appointed to a new post of Commercial Director in 1979. Hooper's Commercial empire (including Marketing which until then had been virtually invisible) was a principal client for Publicity as part of his wider portfolio and his fearsome reputation ensured increasingly frequent meetings behind closed doors trying to come to terms with his multiple and bullying demands. One such demand was to employ Sotheby's to value and dispose of London Transport's world famous poster and art archive. The initial inspection took place under a heavy veil of secrecy and (according to my informant at the time) such was the enormity and importance of the collection, Sotheby's refused to offer a value or to handle a sale. The proposal was abandoned.

Occasionally, as a driver who seldom frequented local pubs at lunchtime, I would be required to chauffeur Hooper from Publicity to the Foote, Cone & Belding advertising agency in Baker Street or back to 55 Broadway. Chief Officers and Directors would be allocated a car for their personal use and professional chauffeurs were available. Ford Granada Ghias for the exalted, Ford Cortinas and Ford Escorts for lesser luminaries, all nominally garaged at Vandon Street close to Broadway. Usually such excursions were conducted in silence but, stuck in an interminable traffic jam on one occasion, the great man asked me what might improve transport in London. My well rehearsed thoughts on simple zonal tickets for bus, tube and trains were explained. Hooper was infuriated with my banal idea and the rest of the journey as the car inched down Baker Street reverted to stony silence. A few years later, the zonal fares and Capitalcards were introduced as a result of GLC's initiatives.

The irony of senior management being chauffeured here and there, to home and then work again, and self drive for lesser grandees, avoiding the inconvenience and unpleasantness of using the system they managed, wasn't lost on me, and neither was it lost on the GLC who terminated the cosy perk. The Conservatives led by Margaret Thatcher were elected to power in 1979 and set about their reforming manifesto with gusto. It was expected that 'reform' of transport would follow in due course, which in the case of the abolishing of express coach licensing happened in October 1980. Reform of London Transport was undoubtedly in the Government's sights.

Poster announcing the London Transport Museum's opening.

Summarising my experiences with London Transport until 1980, it seemed to be a seriously outdated organisation employing people sometimes amazingly good and sometimes quite unemployable. As with any large business, quite a few middle and senior managers rose up the corporate ladder without any trace at all. The very nature of its objectives in serving London's population reliably and efficiently seemed forgotten by many and its senior staff were often totally out of touch with the needs and desires of their paymasters, the travelling public, and of course their relatively new political masters, the Greater London Council. The ghost of Frank Pick (London Transport's former Chief Executive) ruled with a rod of iron but I would think the great man would have been horrified with the many diminished standards prevailing in the 1970s and 1980s.

I was promoted to join London Transport Museum on 2 January 1980 as its Retail Manager. This was a very different experience. Gone were the sometimes stultifying working environments usually encountered. The small management team was largely drawn from the Museum world and a sense of personal freedom and responsibility prevailed. The only focus for the new department was to get the Museum completed and operational by 28 March. The working days became longer and more frenzied. My requests to London Transport's Architects to reconsider certain detailed aspects of the shop design fell on deaf ears. A valuable lesson to employ relevant experts was learned for any future commissioning. The Architect involved had apparently designed what he thought would be suitable without any consultation with operational staff. I organised rudimentary changes with the help of an expert DIY friend and paid for it myself.

The Museum opened on time to great fanfare and a hectic time ensued. London Transport made considerable efforts to galvanise their Press and Publicity machine but within six months the Museum had settled into a rhythm which no longer interested the organisation. The Museum had been set up as a 'Thatcherite' endeavour and after some grant money, was expected to earn its income solely from admissions and shop sales. Shortage of money became a considerable problem and the tightening London Transport finances delivered no respite at all. Consigned to the outer edges of London Transport's solar system, the Museum became woefully impoverished. Vacancies went unfilled for lengthy periods, some key staff worked seven days a week for weeks on end to keep the Museum operational. I, and a couple of others would take the Museum's dilapidated Sherpa van when needed on 'theft' missions to collect spare chairs, desks, office equipment, vehicle spares, saleable shop items and even stationery from contacts made elsewhere in the organisation. This famine of resource went on for some years although there was thankfully a little leeway with staff recruitment. I discovered a loophole in the regulations that didn't expressly forbid employment of 'casual' weekend and holiday staff which we used to great effect to relieve peak season staffing pressure. In due course London Transport took considerable interest in this 'innovation' as it did with the Museum's interpretation of supplier's contracts and a number of other pay and conditions matters, notably among them the vexing issue of unsocial hours payments which had become an organisational minefield with differing conditions across different disciplines within London Transport. Easily forgotten now, but to get a mortgage, only basic salary was ever taken into account and any additional regular payments were disallowed which for a sizeable number of staff on rostered 'unsocial' hours contracts made mortgages unobtainable. Perhaps the Museum was in the forefront of propelling a change to consolidated salaries and the often derided employment of 'casual' labour. Again, London Transport was entirely reactive to events and changing circumstances. The Museum remained for some years in an impoverished state and the slow and inexorable decline of the system continued but its material effects were not felt at the Museum. We were at the hard, sharp end of economy already.

The 1979 Greater London Council election returned a Labour administration and after a brutal 'coup d'etat' removed the newly elected Andrew Macintosh and replaced him with Ken Livingstone, whose central policy was to introduce a cheap integrated zonal based fare system for buses and tubes. The vicissitudes of the ensuing battles between GLC, Government and the principal complainant about the policy, (London Borough of Bromley) through the Courts are well documented. London Transport's finances resulting from huge fares increases following the High Court judgement and seriously diminished passenger usage was now precarious. From the distance of the Museum, the effect was dispiriting and eradicated hope of ever improving Museum fortunes.

On 18 November 1987, a few of us finished work late as usual and readily decided on a few drinks in a local pub. Memorably the air was filled with a cacophony of sirens and we knew something awful must have happened. The Kings Cross fire that fateful evening changed London Transport for ever. A carelessly discarded cigarette on a wooden escalator resulted in an inferno and 31 deaths. The resulting Fennell Inquiry was excoriating. Inept management, poor maintenance, woeful staff training and years of underfunding were its eagerly reported conclusions. The ensuing two years were turbulent for London Transport. Everything changed, sometimes with great haste and sometimes slowly and methodically.

Again the Museum watched from afar as little affected us except for the disappearance of some senior management we had become used to dealing with and reorganisations for which we had to forge rapid new relationships. Bus decentralisation was already in full swing and the bloated and inefficient Chiswick and Aldenham operations closed, but it was the Underground that was swept up in the biggest upheavals.

Major clashes between the GLC and the Thatcher government led to the abolishing of the former and the total reorganisation of London Transport to open its services up to competition. A campaign leaflet issued by the GLC in 1984 is illustrated.

A welcome sight on a dark night

...catch the Night Bus

London Transport operate a network of Night Buses
right through the small hours.
Ring 01-222 1234 any time, night (or day).
and ask for details.

Let's make the most of London

One of a series of well designed posters for the expansion of night
services in 1984.

Andrew Scott had been appointed as Museum Director in 1987 and adroitly repositioned the Museum within the turmoil as a permanent and reliable 'good news' story for London Transport who by this time was particularly eager for any decent press coverage. This turn of events wasn't entirely positive however. London Transport had been forced to divest itself of non-core businesses and a secret plan to dispose of the Museum had been agreed. Talks had taken place with the forerunner of Department for Culture, Media and Sport for the Science Museum to assume control. The main obstacles were financial (as always). The point was reached where I was despatched to addresses around the country to gather Trustees' signatures for the final legal papers for presentation at a precise time late in the evening at London Transport's lawyers in the City. Just how nearly the Museum passed to a new owner I don't know, but the urgency and secrecy felt terribly close to being a reality.

'Publicity' had been retitled to Advertising & Publicity and moved to within the Broadway complex and staffed by much more eager and modern professionals together with some remaining former staff who had mostly been sufficiently 're-educated' to withstand the new excitements and remain in post a while longer. With a former advertising agency executive, Nick Lewis, in charge, it was hoped design standards would improve commensurate with the fashionable modernity of the time. Sadly this wasn't the case and the general output (in fairness as much to do with its principal 'client' Marketing) was as visually nondescript as it had become since the arrival of Hooper. When Hooper left, his replacement was Dr Henry Fitzhugh who found the overall quality of some Underground station environments quite shocking. Fitzhugh's simple initiative to cheaply improve the often intimidating platforms was to commission artists (many were Royal Academicians) and fill the black paper wastelands with vibrant beautiful posters.

Fortunately for me (and the Museum) Fitzhugh was generous with his time and budgets and the Museum benefited hugely from his largesse. Countless thousands of posters were supplied for us to sell. This singularly wonderful programme, almost always only used on commercial 'filler' sites, diminished in the early 1990s as a privatised Commercial Advertising Department sold ever more space. After Fitzhugh departed the programme sadly ceased.

One consequence of the upheavals was the decision to create a new Design Directorate which given the slow and steady decline in design standards was excellent news. Jeremy Rewse-Davis, another new recruit was appointed Design Director and he and his staff began the process of improving every aspect of London Transport's design portfolio generally with very pleasing results. The Museum benefited hugely and for the first time since 1980, we felt part of a wider commercially-driven team. During the latter part of the 1990s, our income rose substantially with posters and products produced with the active support of Design and Marketing. London Transport used the Museum as a corporate showcase in the way they always should have. The Museum, by now ably headed by Sam Mullins, was now a department within the general mainstream of London Transport's world.

London Transport was by then in a better shape than at any time for decades. Passengers, rapidly increasing in number, were treated as customers and 'valued'. The Jubilee line extension was under construction with its wonderful new stations, tube stations and trains were undergoing refurbishment, buses were more reliable and the fare structures sensible and increasingly co-ordinated. Institutional inefficiencies were being eradicated. It had taken one tragic event to effect (or at least accelerate) the necessary change.

5 CHAIRING THE GLC TRANSPORT COMMITTEE
Dave Wetzel

My story on London buses starts in the 1960s when I was a bus conductor and union official. I subsequently became a driver and then an inspector. After being a political organiser for the London Co-operative Society between 1974 and 1981, I became Labour member for Hammersmith and Fulham on the Greater London Council in 1981. Under the leadership of Ken Livingstone I was elected by the Council to be chair of the GLC's Transport Committee that year and until 1986. Later, I was appointed as vice chair of Transport for London between 2000 and 2008, and chair of London Buses from 2000 to 2001. It is my time on the GLC that I will cover in this chapter, but I learned a lot from working on the buses, especially about human nature. I preferred being a conductor as it gave me contact with people. In the driver's cab you were isolated from the public. Some staff preferred this.

The Managing Director of London Buses once told me "the LT Board were quite embarrassed when you became Transport Chair because we thought you would have more knowledge about running buses than we did". At a tactical level that was probably true, but at a strategic level I had a lot to learn. I'd been a councillor for four years from 1964 but I was so far to the left of the Labour Group in control of Hounslow, they didn't even trust me to be vice-chair of their burials committee lest I rouse the dead with copies of Karl Marx and Henry George.

When Ken first asked me to seek election to the GLC, I said: 'No - they're all stuffed shirts wearing pinstripe suits, even the Labour ones, why would I want to get involved with that?' He said: 'No Dave, we're going to have a revolution and you have got to be part of it'.

As a result I was lucky to be selected for Hammersmith North. When we won the election, some of us new Labour members astonished the older GLC Members when we arrived each day in our jeans and check shirts but Ken was always immaculately dressed in his khaki safari suit.

One of my first tasks as Chair was to approve the GLC's draft TPP (Transport Policies and Programmes) a policy document submitted to Whitehall each year to qualify for government grants. I had only a weekend to read this huge volume. I went through it thoroughly reading every word and made changes with my usual red pen (I always signed every letter in red - "Yours for Socialism"). One line in the draft TPP stood out like a sore thumb "In London there is a secular decline in bus use" I struck this out and wrote NO! I don't care whether it is secular or religious - by lowering fares,

improving services and controlling traffic growth we will get More Bums on Seats!".

To ensure we worked together as a team I held regular meetings of all the Labour members of the transport committee, I called this our Transport Collective where Paul Moore was much more than a Vice-Chair, I described him as the brains of the Collective and we really worked as co-chairs for the whole five years. Paul Moore did an excellent job promoting cycling, walking, green traffic management, road safety, bus lanes and other bus priority measures.

One of my first decisions was to scrap the Conservatives' overtime ban which led to an immediate increase in bus services on all routes across London, we also operated more Underground train miles. I made a commitment to stick to the fares cut and the other transport promises in the manifesto we had been elected on. Our manifesto wasn't perfect: for example, it was pretty silent on the question of disability and transport, but that was not a bad thing because it gave us free rein to introduce many improvements for people with disabilities. Consultations showed that one of the main things required was an extension of the Dial-a-Ride network from three boroughs to the whole of London under the management of disabled people themselves. As well as some physical improvements to buses and the Underground making them more helpful for people with disabilities, we also introduced Taxicard offering cheaper rides by cab and experimented with wheelchair-accessible taxis.

An early initiative of ours was the introduction of bus passes; we then went on to make them cheaper. More importantly we also later introduced the Travelcard, giving travel on both buses and the Underground. My biggest regret is that we never got the Travelcard down to the price of a bus pass. I remember being with Peter Hendy years later when one day on a bus in Hayes we spoke to someone who had travelled from Abbey Wood by bus. He was doing this journey every day. I asked him why he was doing this all by bus rather than using rail and he said he could not afford the Travelcard. It seems silly that we give an incentive for people to travel on a less efficient system than rail. One of the regrets when we reduced fares was that we couldn't include British Rail. We did not control BR and the Thatcher Government told them they would lose government grant if they accepted GLC money to cut their fares in line with the Underground.

One of the first problems with bus operation I addressed was the shortage of staff and the corresponding gaps in service. When I was a bus inspector I would check the rosters a few days before operation and see gaps where staff were not available, meaning that some passengers would be having to wait 30 or 45 minutes for their bus. In some cases, three or four buses in sequence were cut. I made it my business to ask and persuade crews to accept overtime to make sure we had as many peak hour journeys operating as possible.

At the GLC I wanted to schedule the services for the bus staff LT actually employed, rather than the invisible establishment number, then we would have had a service that was much more reliable. I wanted to keep the establishment number and employ more staff when possible to reduce the headways. Unfortunately, the union always blocked this, understandably saying that we should increase the wages to get the staff needed rather than reduce the services to match the staff we had. It was only as a by-product of the Law Lords, under their December 1981 ruling, making us reverse our fares reduction under Fares Fair that we were able in September 1982 to impose schedule reductions that enabled us to operate a much more reliable service.

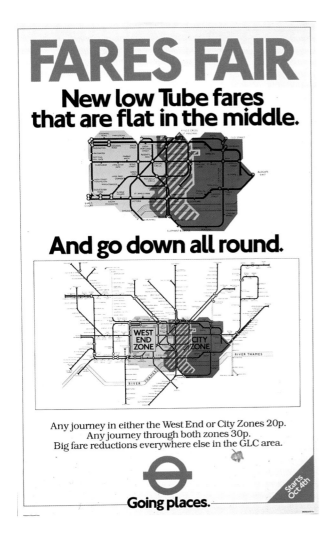

During this period, we got Phil Goodwin at Oxford University to do a study of the night buses. The night buses had traditionally been used to serve the dock workers and night workers printing newspapers in Fleet Street. By the early 1980s the night bus routes bore no resemblance to the needs of a 24-hour city. Phil Goodwin came up with the idea of having a spider's web of night bus routes all originating from Trafalgar Square and going out into the suburbs. Unfortunately, the way to pay for this improvement was to introduce one person operation and even though we would employ more extra bus drivers than the conductors we lost, the Union delayed the introduction of this huge improvement by six months. Thanks to this initiative, today we have many daytime bus routes that have been changed to 24-hour services. This also helped with the night-time parking of buses in TfL days when we doubled the night bus service. Because LT had closed and sold so many bus garages, we were being forced to park buses on the streets – far better to keep the buses on the routes and employ drivers to provide a 24-hour service.

Prior to 1981 bus fares had always been graduated, so that the further you travelled the more you paid. We looked at other options and then went out to public consultation. What we really wanted was something similar to the French carte orange travelcard, introduced there in 1975. London Transport made it clear that was too big a step to make in one go. I was told that under the Horace Cutler (Conservative) regime in the late 1970s the GLC had suggested that a carte orange scheme be introduced and London Transport said it was impossible in London and demanded that the GLC take out any references to possible carte orange schemes from committee reports. I've never understood why the Tories so meekly conformed when in fact they were the policy makers, not LT.

However, we had included the carte orange proposal in our 1981 manifesto and to London Transport's credit they came up with a leap forward towards that system; a zonal fare structure. After public consultation, we introduced this together with an overall reduction of 32% in total fares in October 1981. We called this "Fares Fair".

To avoid a fares increase just before the 1981 GLC elections the Conservative administration froze London Transport fares leaving a revenue shortfall that we had to address. Consequently our supplementary rate in October 1981 had to pay for four items: One the Conservative revenue gap; two our improvements to services and three Fares Fair; this totalled over £100m to be paid by London ratepayers. The fourth item had nothing to do with funding transport but arose because central government under Margaret Thatcher disapproved of our transport policies and took away some of the government's rate support, leaving us to find another 70p for every extra £1 we spent on London Transport. This led to the well-known challenge in the courts by Bromley Council against the rates increase. Bromley has mainline but no Underground so the Conservative councillors objected to their residents paying. The GLC won the first hearing at the High Court. Bromley appealed however and at the Court of Appeal under Lord Denning we lost. This came as a big shock. We knew that Bromley had tried to get other councils in the London area to contribute towards the costs for their challenge but no other Borough was willing to support it because they also thought it wouldn't win.

Before the Denning judgement, our lawyers had said we had nothing to worry because Parliament's London Transport Act (1969) had clearly stated that the GLC could give a grant to London Transport for any purpose. I went to the House of Lords on 17 December 1981 to hear them judicate in Bromley's favour. I said this was purely a political judgement and described The Law Lords as 'vandals in ermine' because they were causing more damage to the public transport system than any group of yobbos could ever achieve. The Law Lords were only concerned about the interests of property owners their judgement showed no care for traffic congestion, the reduction in accidents and pollution. Their ruling was that London Transport had a fiduciary duty to the ratepayers to run the system efficiently and economically, and their interpretation of 'efficiently and economically' was that London Transport should maximise their income and increase fares to the point of diminishing returns. The immediate response was to double fares in March 1982 but Ken Livingstone, Paul Moore, John McDonnell myself and other left-wing GLC members opposed this but we were outvoted by Tories, right-wing Labour and the Lib/Dems.

There were public demonstrations against the judgement and one of them led by Mary and Derek Evans involved a whole group of people with carrier bags filling a bus at its West Hampstead starting point on the 159 route which went across Westminster Bridge. As soon as they left the stand, they opened

their carrier bags and took out judge's wigs, made from carpets, and red silk capes. They said: 'we are judges and we are hijacking this bus to take to Westminster'. The "hijacked" bus was met by supporters and the press when they arrived at County Hall.

The GLC ran a legal 'Keep Fares Fair' campaign but all of its material had to be assessed by lawyers in advance. We made up a drawing of a judge smashing up a concrete roundel with a hammer. The lawyers said 'you can't use that, it's too strong' so we gave it to the unions for them to use for a leaflet. I'm sure that the ridicule heaped on the judges by their contempt for democracy influenced their decision to eventually reverse the Law Lords.

Some of us also ran the 'Can't Pay, Won't Pay' campaign (CPWP). We created CPWP tickets on which we added our names and addresses instructing LT to come and collect the fare from our address. We would give the "ticket" to the conductor. London Transport ignored most of these tickets only contacting a few of us repeat offenders (about 17) and took us to court as an example. Beforehand, an inspector had come round to my home in Hounslow to deliver the court summons, as my wife and I continued the 'Can't Pay, Won't Pay' protest for some time. I invited him in for tea and cake. He said that they had drawn lots to see who would

come round to my house to suffer my ire; he did not expect to get such a friendly welcome. I pointed out that it was part of a political protest and I needed my day in court to get the message across.

One day, travelling back to County Hall on a number 12 bus, on seeing my CPWP ticket the conductor refused to ring the bell at Trafalgar Square. I explained the reason for the delay to the passengers in the lower saloon and they all voted that I should stay on the bus but upstairs they voted for me to leave the bus. My comment back at County Hall was: "Never trust the smokers on the top deck of a Routemaster!".

To prepare for my second time in court (after the magistrate accused me of behaving like an animal) I went to see Sir Peter Hall at the National Theatre. I wanted to borrow a monkey costume I could wear. His costume manager didn't have a monkey costume but loaned me a large gorilla used as a ventriloquist's dummy. This was better, because you could see both me and the monkey in court. I put "Tom" (after Lord "Tom Denning") into a plastic bag under the dock during the lunch break. When my time came, I put my hand up the dummy so I could turn its head and roll his eyes while the magistrate tried to ignore what was happening. It was in the dock with me for about two or three minutes before a policeman took it off me.

The magistrate asked if I had committed the offence as charged. I began my answer by giving a lengthy history of the GLC's election win with and its manifesto, the Keep Fares Fair campaign and all the things that felt relevant to the action we had taken. He interrupted me and repeated his question. I then resumed speaking about my reasons for the campaign and ultimately, he walked out of the court, as he took my comments as a refusal to answer his question. I leapt onto his dais and banging his gavel on the desk, to a cheer from our supporters in the public gallery, I declared "All the Can't Payers – Won't Payers innocent!". Following discussions with an usher it was agreed that I could continue speaking for fifteen minutes about the reasons for our campaign (a million Londoners' votes worth more than the votes of the five Law Lords) and then answer the question. Along with others in the court that day I was fined for my part.

Camden Council later approached me about the possibility of them challenging the GLC for ignoring the Greater London Development Plan when doubling London Transport's fares. I welcomed their suggestion and consulted the public on a "Balanced Plan" which cut fares by 25% but also introduced the Travelcard which I had wanted in 1981. In October 1982 we instructed LT to reduce bus and train fares but they refused, citing the Law Lords' Judgement as to why it would be illegal. We dismissed the lawyers who had defended Fairs Fare and appointed Roger Henderson QC, who not only represented us in court but also oversaw and advised amendments on every report we took to Committee on the fares policy. We won the case in the High Court and London Transport did not appeal as they also wanted to cut fares and introduce Travelcards. In the outturn the Travelcard was more successful than any of us had anticipated, and because of the additional sales meant a lower subsidy to LT than expected.

The Thatcher government extended our term of office by one year but finally abolished us in 1986. As a postscript to all this, when I had lunch with London Transport chairman Sir Peter Masefield just before his retirement in 1982, he said: 'one piece of advice, Dave, never introduce free fares as we couldn't cope with the demand'. I said that was the point: increase staff and increase the services to cope with the demand, and reduce traffic to make the roads safer, cleaner and more efficient. For our draft 1981 manifesto the Labour Party had originally included the idea of road pricing but it was felt that London was not ready for that. Later though, I thought this was a mistake. It would probably have given us the money for Fares Fair without all the legal problems that followed. Later, when Ken became Mayor of London and I was Vice-Chair of the TfL Board, Ken bravely introduced the Central London Congestion Charge Scheme – despite huge opposition it proved to be a huge success.

6 ESTABLISHING THE LRT TENDERED BUS UNIT
Nick Newton

Tensions between the Conservative Government and the Labour-controlled Greater London Council led to the London Regional Transport Act 1984 which took control of London Transport from the GLC and passed it to the Secretary of State for Transport.

The Act, and the subsequent letter of objectives from the Secretary of State required LRT to "provide or *secure* the provision of public transport services" and obliged LRT to "invite the *submission of tenders* for certain activities where it is thought appropriate" – the **core statutory obligations**.

Section 4 of the Act imposed on LRT a duty to establish major subsidiary operating companies – London Buses Limited (LBL) and London Underground Limited (LUL) so that they could be run on more business lines.

LRT's Group Planning with added commercial and procurement expertise were tasked with developing a proposal to deliver these new obligations as a matter of urgency. They addressed the challenge independent from the embedded monopolistic comfort and deficiencies which characterised the bus organisation and its performance.

With the Board pressing for quick results, within three months the small dedicated team brought forward a succinct but comprehensive proposal backed by a clearly thought through analysis and rationale.

Four key elements of an appropriate bus tendering system were defined:

What we would buy was determined by the requirements of the *core statutory obligations* which demanded that in ensuring an *integrated service network* LRT would specify the services to be provided (route, frequencies, first and last journeys, size of vehicle) in precise detail. It was also proposed that LRT's *full fare and ticketing arrangements* would apply with bus operators responsible for all data and revenue collected on LRT's behalf.

Strong competition would be essential for successful and sustainable tendering. Two key principles were pursued – independence from LBL and fairness.

For decades LT had effectively been a monopoly reinforced by its approach to its service licensing powers where the "public interest" test had evolved into the "LT's interest" test when considering operator proposals to operate their own bus services. Consequently, as LRT tackled market creation, many prospective bidders (particularly from the private sector) had direct experience of exclusion and were suspicious of LRT's motives.

The team had to work hard to convince prospects that they were wholly committed to establishing an honest, high quality process and were entirely independent of LBL.

This independence was supported to some extent by LBL's evident public resistance to what was emerging (although some of the more enlightened senior LBL folk could see merit in a competitive tendering system helping them in addressing the major deficiencies of the bus operations where there was poor service quality delivered at a high cost).

In addition to establishing a clear independence the other key to establishing tendering's credibility with an embryonic market had to be the offer of a realistic and balanced commercial proposition.

The Commercial and Tendering Proposition was developed from these two principles and determined the other key elements of the contract.

Firstly, bidders would tender their costs and margins for operating the specified service (their major exposure) with LRT retaining the revenue risk. Operators would, however, be responsible for the effective collection of all revenues.

LBL would be allowed to bid to retain their services but their tenders were required to be transparent and to reflect all relevant costs (i.e. no hidden or cross subsidy). These requirements would be reinforced by the independent Tendering Unit being obliged to seek LRT internal audit scrutiny of any LBL bid they were not entirely comfortable with.

Independent analysis of current operators/potential bidders indicated a number of shared characteristics:
- operating bases on the fringes of Greater London;
- operations largely comprising commercial coach operations with a significant volume of daily hire;
- the prime characteristic of their commercial dealings was high margins but high debt and cash flow risk. Many spent considerable time chasing debtors;
- limited access to capital funds;
- relatively small fleet sizes, predominantly coaches;

This data determined two further key essentials of a proposition targeted at attracting new bidders.

Firstly, the early services to be offered for tender would be on the London periphery near to operator bases.

Secondly contract payment arrangements would provide a secure and attractive cash flow in stark contrast to the prevailing situation with most operators we were striving to attract. In effect this was overtly targeted at offering an "antidote" to the generally high margin / high risk existing business.

Part of the proposition with a 75% of the 4 weekly contract payment being paid directly into the operators' bank by direct debit was completely unprecedented in LRT and explicit authority to adopt it was obtained from the Chairman. (A separate programme of payments were set up – this was the balance of 25% which was adjusted for penalties before being paid also every four weeks but timed to be two weeks apart from the larger payment)

The impact was significant and is believed to have been, possibly, the single most important contributor to the achievement of multiple competitive bids on all tendering from the first group onwards.

Private operators were able to bid for the (typically) 3-year contracts with success giving them a guaranteed payment every two weeks over the entire 3 years. Provision was also made for contract prices to track inflation to protect operators.

The contractual service timetable annual mileage and the annual contract price would produce an average price per mile which would be the deduction made from contract payments for each mile not operated. Mileage lost due to traffic conditions was not deducted in the first year (more on this later).

Electronic ticket machines (Wayfarer was selected after an evaluation process) would be free issued to operators and LRT revenue inspectors would monitor operators' revenue collection activities.

Fully compliant bids were mandatory but bidders could offer alternative proposals. The selection of the successful bid would be based on best value not lowest price. The proposed contract document was crafted applying procurement and commercial legal expertise and represented a balanced proposition. In particular the principle of risk falling where it could best be managed was key.

Initially a small group set about devising a comprehensive arrangement to ensure that the successful bidders delivered on all their contractual obligations – the embryonic Tendered Bus Unit (TBU) was established. It later became a 'Division' rather than a 'Unit'.

Joining me was John Wood from the LRT Commercial office, Marina Ainsworth from the Purchasing Section and in due course Malcolm Wren from Group Planning became a permanent member of the team.

A range of monitoring systems were needed to cover operational performance (quantity and quality), fare collection and revenue payment and "regulatory and safety" compliance.

Whilst these generic areas were covered by existing LBL and Planning systems imagination and clarity of thought was required to devise robust, effective and transparent variants to reinforce the integrity of the tendering activity.

Examples of what was achieved were:

Revenue inspection: LBL's revenue inspection system was independent of their bus operations and processes were robust. However, in order to create a contractually legitimate process, trusted by private operators, that could support a regime of "fines" to operators for poor or inappropriate revenue collection a statistically robust sampling rate of on bus checks by both uniformed and plain clothes inspectors was essential. An appropriate formal contract was established between the TBU and the Revenue Protection department.

Revenue payments: In addition to the scrutiny of on bus revenue collection there was a need to establish that actual cash collected on bus was registered and the correct amounts paid to TBU by operators.

This was achieved by the use of the Wayfarer electronic ticket machines by all operators which captured all fares transactions securely on cassettes which were uploaded to a depot pc and delivered overnight to TBU.

A subsequent development of this system was the implementation of a bespoke IT system which trawled the depot pcs overnight and transferred all data to TBU's system. Only when the data was transferred were operators able to access it.

Engineering standards: Tensions between TBU and LBL arose on the issue of engineering standards on vehicle maintenance by private operators. The suggestion was that private operators applied lower standards than LBL albeit they still complied with statutory requirements. It was suggested that, as LBL standards were in excess of statutory ones, these same standards should apply to non LBL operators.

TBU resisted this proposal. It was logical that ALL operators would have "internal" standards above regulatory and statutory ones in order to establish a "margin for error" and this mirrored what LBL were doing.

Furthermore, the implications of LRT implying that statutory standards were not acceptable could have created complications. TBU prevailed but to reinforce its position it contracted with LBL's semi-independent Engineering function to conduct arranged and "surprise" audits of depot activities with all operators.

One of the first inspections of one of the private operators was reported as revealing materially higher standards than LBL.

The first bidding tranche was a group of outer suburban routes in localities where research indicated a number of smaller bus and coach operators had based their depots.

The services were relatively small in terms of route length and operating resources required (buses

London Buslines was one of the first six operators to win a contract to run a London bus service. Former London Transport DM 1007 is shown.

and staff) and, generally, did not have any significant operating challenges. Later we became increasingly confident and major trunk London bus routes were added to the tendering programme.

Competitive bids were received for all routes from the LBL incumbents, current and former National Bus Company subsidiaries and a handful of private operators. All bids were, as required, fully compliant which was a strong indication that the commercial proposition was well thought through.

Around half of the contracts were awarded to the incumbent LBL companies with the remainder going to current and former NBC subsidiaries and private operators.

Before results were cleared a number of the "successful" LBL bids were referred by TBU to LRT Audit resulting in a small number of disqualifications.

The first tendered services started operations on Saturday 13 July 1985 with the balance of the first tranche commencing on subsequent Saturdays. There was significant industry interest in this pioneering step. Despite warnings of dire consequences, and with no previous experience to draw on, the services with new operators started well with only a few teething problems.

Performance was generally acceptable within a short time and further tranches of routes were announced soon after.

By the end of the financial year 56 routes had been competitively tendered: 26 of them to London Buses; 22 of them were awarded to National Bus Company subsidiaries; and eight to others.

In the first couple of years the Tendered Bus Unit

(later Division) overran its cost budget for the very best of reasons. The services now being provided under contract were running rather more of their scheduled mileage than had been anticipated...

A number of lessons were learned in the early years: some bidders underestimated the task of running an intensive bus service day in and day out and did not have sufficient resource. The reliability of some of the secondhand buses used turned out to be poor, and London Buses was found on more than one occasion to have incorrectly apportioned costs to secure tender wins by tinkering with the cost allocations of its 'block grant' services.

The Tendered Bus Division demonstrated its muscle in 1988 when London Country North East staff went on strike and all the contracts were terminated and reassigned.

Early choices of routes for tendering were those with poor financial performance but it became clear that this was not entirely ideal because the loss of one route inside a London Buses garage still meant the overhead cost had to be recovered and as that burden became shared over a smaller set of routes their own tender prices were having to rise.

It followed then that attempts were made to put out to contract groups of routes in one area. Indeed, despite all the random effects on the tendering programme over 35 years those early networks like Bexleyheath and Sutton can still be observed together in the tendering schedule. In some cases – such as Bexleyheath, Harrow and Orpington newly created 'low cost' London Buses units succeeded at the bidding stage whereas the consequences for Loughton and later Hornchurch and Walthamstow were terminal.

Since more than 50% of all bus operating costs are wages, it is no surprise that the private sector did so well with staff employed on less restrictive contracts – the most significant of this was a maximum working day being the legal limit rather than the much shorter one enjoyed by London Transport staff. The low cost units set up inside London Buses attempted to counteract this but again in some cases it went too far. A wholesale optimisation of schedules at Bexleybus meant staff working on different routes inside the same working day. It sounds more enjoyable and less monotonous but in practice whenever there were serious delays, incidents or staff cuts, the consequences rippled across the whole local network as staff were not in the right position for their reliefs or changeovers.

The Trade Union was strongly opposed to the whole concept of outsourcing and what they saw as privatisation. They struggled to develop an effective resistance.

The make-up of the tendering programme, particularly its very modest start, made it difficult to identify a "target" on which to focus their resistance (the majority of their members considered themselves to be unaffected by the small groups of routes being tendered).

More significant was the view adopted by most bus operating staff that for them individually tendering offered them an opportunity to benefit from more interesting and flexible working if the routes were retained or a generous redundancy pay out if the work was lost (London Buses' severance arrangements dictated that those with the longest service would be at the front of the queue for pay out) coupled with the prospect of moving to the successful bidder on different terms but similar take home pay.

Some minor industrial action occurred which had little effect. The first significant action arose after the award of the large network operated out of Walthamstow garage to the London Buses Forest Company incumbent.

This "win" was on the basis of a radical new pay and operating package which the Union rejected resulting in the contracts going to an alternative group of private operators. The Union called a well supported strike at Walthamstow but it failed fairly quickly when the Tendered Bus Unit brought in emergency operating contracts with other operators.

When tendering was first set up in the 1980s it was widely criticised from all sides – within London Transport, by the Trades Union, and by local politicians. In 1990 Newham MP the late Tony Banks accused the Government of a 'fiddle' over the award of route 24 to Grey Green. But over time and as tendering grew what became clear is that significant cost savings were being achieved and performance was growing. It was therefore no surprise that in 1993 London Transport announced that the 55% of the network which still had not been subject to competitive tendering would be shifted to individual route contracts by negotiation and which would join a London-wide tendering programme based on a new plan.

Despite many changes in the market – the privatisation of London Buses, changes in market dynamics, fluctuating political directions – from driving down cost to adding volume, passenger ridership growth and changing financial fortunes, the basics of the system laid down in 1984 with Gross Cost contracts, private sector taking the appropriate risks, with what is now TfL managing the network have endured now for over 35 years.

The base originally set up by Stagecoach near Stratford for its part of its East London operations.

7 THE TRIALS OF TICKETING
Roger Torode

Fare collection was always a major challenge for London's bus operators. The employment of conductors to collect the fares, inspectors to check on passengers and conductors, garage staff to count the cash, security in the garage and for transit to the bank, and the associated bank charges were an immense cost. There was temptation at every stage to those handling the cash, and the need for checks and investigations to ensure that it was done honestly - which it wasn't always.

The scale of this task was huge. When decimalisation came in 1971, it was estimated that LT handled 80% of the coins circulating in London every week, and 68 tons of 6d coins were stockpiled to enable a smooth transition to the new currency, with all fares in units of 6d (2.5p).

The slow collection of fares on One-Person-Operated buses (OPO) led to London retaining conductors for many years after other cities had dispensed with them - if central London services had been converted to OPO, they would have been slowed down so much that more buses would have been needed to maintain the frequency of service, which would have cancelled

out the savings from OPO. There were experiments with two-stream boarding using turnstiles and ticket cancellers, but none were found to be satisfactory for widespread use throughout London.

In the 1980s, manufacturers were beginning to introduce electronic ticket machines. These were much faster to operate, greatly simplified the job of bus drivers and provided far more management information on the tickets issued, including where and when they were sold.

Tests of drivers' ticket machines

In 1984, I moved within LT to the Operations Systems Department of London Buses and began to look at the Electronic Ticket Machines (ETMs) that were coming onto the market. There were three UK manufacturers to consider. London Buses felt a responsibility to give them all a chance to show what they had to offer, and we started to evaluate them and run operational trials of machines that might prove suitable - the aim would then be to choose one machine for the entire London OPO fleet.

We also looked at other ways of dealing with cash

Boarding speeds on OPO buses were unacceptably slow and conductors were retained in London for many years more than in other cities. A Titan on route 212 boards at Walthamstow Central in 1982 - passengers arrived more quickly than they could board the bus, and long queues developed.

New tickets on Routes 26, 125, 221, N13 and N21. Starting 8th April.

A new type of ticket machine is being tested on pay-as-you-enter buses operating from Finchley Garage on Routes 26, 125, 221, N13 and N21.

Instead of showing the fare paid as a code letter, your ticket will indicate the actual amount paid in figures.

Please retain it for inspection as usual.

Publicity for the trial Wayfarer ticket machines at Finchley. (Roger Torode collection)

fare payments. We visited Belfast and Stockholm where the drivers 'bought' cash fare tickets in bulk from the operator, sold them to passengers and used the proceeds to buy more tickets, but this was not thought practical in London.

So we ran three trials, the Wayfarer at Finchley, the Almex Timtronic at Loughton, and the Control Systems Farestram at Palmers Green, each replacing the existing mechanical machines on all the OPO buses in the garage. Each system had a free-standing computer to manage the ticket machines and provide data for the garage staff to feed into the LT finance system.

Wayfarer were a new company who had a successful track record with shop cash registers. They had thoroughly researched the bus market and produced a new machine to match what was wanted. They were impressive in their demonstrations, arriving with travel bags containing several machines, memory modules and a full depot system. This would all be up and running in a few minutes so that we could work through the whole operation, issuing tickets, downloading our modules, and then seeing those tickets on the depot computer. They already had the system in use with a number of UK operators and we visited Eastbourne to learn from their experience. It was an attractive system, simple, straightforward and robust - and it was interesting to note that our trial of the system in one London garage was bigger than Eastbourne's fleet implementation!

Almex were the supplier of the existing mechanical machines on London's OPO buses. They sold ticketing systems throughout the world and knew their business, remarking that there were more buses in

London than there were in Australia. Their Timtronic machine worked well though it was large and complex - but it deserved to be tested.

Control Systems of Uxbridge were developing their Farestram machine. They were a long-standing manufacturer of transport ticket equipment, going back to the Bell Punch. Their proposed machine looked good, but it needed development and this was taking them time to achieve. They insisted it would be ready for our trials and it was felt right to give them the opportunity, but they were not well organised and their progress was slow - for example, they had chosen an aluminium module casing from Switzerland that was severely delayed, and the machine software also took a long time to get right. On one occasion, during a technical meeting at their Uxbridge HQ, the Chief Engineer suddenly got up, said that it was his Bridge night, and left the meeting!

The Wayfarer trial at Finchley Garage started on 8 April 1985, the Almex trial at Loughton on 7 May, and the Control Systems Farestram finally went into service at Palmers Green on 11 November 1985. These were all Mondays or the Tuesday after a Bank Holiday, so fitting the buses took place over the weekend ready for the next morning's runout. LBL's technical team worked with the garage staff, with the manufacturer in attendance.

There were the inevitable small glitches at first - a Finchley driver came back off his first bus saying the clock in his machine had raced ahead to August, so he was now off on his summer holiday! Almex had a favourite story about the driver, outside London, who accidently issued sixty 2p tickets instead of two 60p tickets, and during the first evening at Palmers

'Passengers' recruited for the afternoon board one of the trial buses at Chiswick works. This is the swipe reader which seemed promising but proved too difficult for many passengers to use.

Green a Control Systems technician was heavily engaged in adjusting data from each module which for some reason the Farestram garage computer system was not collecting automatically. But generally, they settled down well and drivers and garage staff liked the systems they were using. We took a few staff from each garage to see the others, with the result that everyone thought their own system was the best.

We learned a great deal about our requirements for the fleet system. The choice of machine was straightforward, since Wayfarer demonstrably had the best product for our requirements, and they worked well with us to meet our needs for the London system. But we had to make them believe that their competitors were credible in order to keep their price down!

Two new Metrobuses were allocated for the trials before release to their garages. They made a short circuit of the Chiswick Works road system between stops to set down and pick up their passengers.

Some of the Ogle design features were incorporated into DMS 2456 which was first used in these trials, before its repaint and re-entry into service.

Fitting the fleet with the Wayfarer

LT had a reputation for designing everything itself rather than buying what was already available from manufacturers, and so London Buses was trying hard to buy off-the-shelf equipment wherever possible. But we also had far more experience of heavy urban operation than smaller operators, with a more demanding working environment, and research teams looking in detail at the operation and finding ways to make it work better. So while we tried to buy a standard Wayfarer, there needed to be improvements - which would also help other operators. The key features we wanted were:

- A change to the keyboard so that the fare descriptors were on a card strip below each row of keys. This could easily be changed when there was a fare change. The original Wayfarer required prising off every key cap and replacing its fare descriptor - impractical on around 4,000 machines across London, all on the same night of the fares change.
- A passenger fare display on top of the machine, to show the passenger the total fare to be paid - and also to allow Revenue Protection staff to see what the driver was doing.
- Software changes, particularly to enable daily reporting of statistics without major changes to the London system.

- Lastly, we were now planning a trial of card readers on OPO buses, to read magnetic tickets as used on the Underground and permit two-stream boarding. The initial software requirements for this were built into the Wayfarer machines.

Wayfarer were proud of their machine, and as these changes were made new versions of the software chip appeared with a code commencing 'LAW'. When I asked what this stood for, the development engineer initially refused to say. Eventually, he admitted that it stood for 'London's Awful Wayfarer'! So we got our 'off the shelf' machine, but with some pretty substantial changes to meet our needs - which we felt made their machine better for everyone.

The project was discussed throughout with the London Bus Committee of the Trade Union, representing the drivers. Negotiations resulted in a reduction in driver signing on and off times because the machine did a number of calculations that drivers had previously done themselves. There were also staff reductions in garages, ticket machine maintenance and in the traffic audit department. This benefit across the fleet was enough to pay for the whole project within a matter of months, so the other benefits, including the improved passenger data were, in effect, "free". A major implementation exercise converted the whole fleet to Wayfarers over the following months, one garage a fortnight.

Autocheck

London Buses was conducting considerable research at the time into bus design led by David Quarmby, the Managing Director Buses, and called the New Omnibus Concepts and Systems programme (NOCS).

Ogle Design of Letchworth carried out the bus design work. The objectives included faster boarding, improved accessibility, and better ergonomics for staff and passengers. Improved fare collection with two cardreaders to permit two-stream boarding was an important part of this. The Underground Ticketing System (UTS), using magnetically-encoded tickets, encouraged the development of a compatible bus system to provide integration between bus and Underground. If all Travelcards, Bus Passes and Pensioner Passes were read by the new system, it would be possible to extend OPO substantially. A number of manufacturers around the world were producing bus equipment that might achieve this.

Two-stream boarding at Woolwich.

I then became Project Manager for the Bus Ticketing System Project, BTS. We initially carried out a series of trials of different cardreaders at Chiswick Works in 1985 and early 1986. Several suppliers expressed interest and loaned equipment that we fitted to two new Metrobuses. These came to us before being allocated to garages, and were driven around a short circuit of the Chiswick road system by two Revenue Protection Inspectors recently promoted from drivers. We recruited 'passengers' for a few hours from the local Job Centre, and they boarded and alighted using the cardreaders. Operational Research staff recorded boarding speeds and observed how easy the readers were to use, and we photographed and filmed the results. If successful, we would move on to a larger trial in passenger service.

There were two types of cardreader supplied by four different manufacturers, a 'swipe-reader' from one, and 'post box' cardreaders from the other three. With the 'swipe-reader', passengers held onto their card whilst swiping it along a slot in the top of the cardreader. This looked attractive as it meant that the passenger kept moving onto the bus and never let go of their card, but it proved too difficult for some passengers to fully insert the card and swipe it consistently at the right speed for the reader to work, and this led to misreads and delays. With the 'post box' reader, the passenger would pause by the cardreader, insert their ticket and wait for it to be returned. This made the 'read' more reliable, though it interrupted the flow of passengers onto the bus.

The 'post box' machines were successful enough for us to proceed to a trial, and the Thamesmead area was chosen as it was reasonably self-contained with most local routes then run from Plumstead garage. Following our Chiswick trials and a tendering exercise, Thorn EMI and Wayfarer were chosen, in both cases linked to the Wayfarer drivers' ticket machine which provided location and time, and collected the data into the driver's module. Plumstead received new Leyland Olympian double-deckers which incorporated some of the Ogle Design features, and these were fitted with two cardreaders, as were some older Leyland Titans and Nationals. All were two-door buses with wide entrances to allow two-stream boarding. The trial was marketed as 'Autocheck', and a range of magnetic tickets, Bus Passes and Travelcards were sold through the network of local bus pass agents, and Pensioner passes were also distributed.

The Thamesmead trial began on 22 March 1987. A major problem emerged very quickly. Daily and weekly tickets were supplied to agents in strips with perforations between each card, and the agent would tear off a card from the strip when selling it to the passenger - this is still standard procedure in many venues which sell tickets from a roll. However, the torn perforations on the card quickly frayed and began to clog the cardreader mechanism, causing it to jam. The machine then had to be swapped on the bus and taken away to be cleared. As a result, a repair workshop was quickly set up in Plumstead Garage, with LBL technical staff at the bus stops outside waiting to swap jammed machines with spare ones to keep everything moving. They soon achieved a speed of less than 90 seconds for a machine swap, and drivers were flashing their headlights as they approached the stop if they had a jammed cardreader. Meanwhile, all the rolls of tickets were recovered from agents and sent back to the manufacturer to have their edges guillotined to remove the perforations, then returned as individual cards to the agents. Where possible, cards already sold were also swapped-out. The problem was resolved, but in the meantime Revenue Protection Inspectors were handing out leaflets to passengers saying 'Sorry' for the inconvenience caused.

The other key lessons learned were, firstly, that the readers need to be kept scrupulously clean inside, with properly aligned internal mechanisms, if they are to work properly This is difficult to achieve when they are fitted to buses which are working up to 18 hours a day and seven days a week, bouncing around on London's roads, with wet, damp, dust and oil to contend with.

Secondly, bus passengers do not always treat their tickets well, perhaps because bus tickets are generally lower value than rail tickets. They often bend or fiddle with them when waiting to board the bus, or hold them in the rain causing the card to expand and jam the cardreader, and then perhaps put it in their back pocket and sit on it, all of which can damage the magnetic track making it difficult or impossible to read.

As the trial continued, tendering of bus services in the Bexley area meant that the scheme was no longer self-contained, as more operators and garages became involved. Some of the buses on the tendered routes had single doors, so that only one cardreader could be fitted, and there could only be single-stream boarding.

The trial settled down and came to work reasonably well technically, but it did not improve boarding speeds much and was clearly not the way forward. The equipment was subsequently removed and ticketing in Thamesmead went back to normal.

At the same time as this work, the Ticketing Working Group of the UK Passenger Transport Executives were conducting a trial in Oldham of stored value ticketing using a bar code system. Passengers put their stored value card in the reader, which read the code, deducted the fare value and issued a new barcode ticket for the remaining amount. I was the LT representative on this group, and Marcus Smith,

MD of London Buses, instructed me to visit Oldham incognito with technical colleagues to see it in action. We went for a day in September 1986 and reported back. We also observed their Almex ticket-canceller system in use - and the number of passengers who were just pretending to use it without inserting their tickets far enough to remove a journey. Marcus Smith fed this information to his senior PTE contacts, neatly damaging my relationship with my PTE opposite numbers who I had been instructed not to tell of the visit!

The bus industry was changing dramatically at this time and I moved to a new job as General Manager of Walthamstow garage, then becoming Commercial Director of the London Forest subsidiary bus company.

Autocheck publicity and tickets.

From March 22nd use AUTOCHECK when you board.

AUTOCHECK –checks your new style Bus Pass, Travelcard or Bus Reader Card as you board-without driver inspection.
Cash and old style passes still accepted by drivers.

Smartcards on route 212

At the end of 1991, I was asked to look into the contactless credit card-size tickets being developed that communicated with the reader by radio. The cardreader was sealed and solid state, and passengers kept hold of their card which they simply touched on the reader, so solving the mechanical problems of the Autocheck system, while the smartcards would be robust and unlikely to be damaged in use. This could be useful in a deregulated bus environment and it justified research and, possibly, a trial scheme. I was to be based in the Tendered Bus Division, where I was given a desk and a phone, and started work.

The LRT Chairman, Sir Wilfrid Newton, was very interested in the concept, which he referred to as 'Stored Value Ticketing'. He expected that bus passengers would have one smartcard to pay their fares on any deregulated London bus, producing transaction data for bus operators to claim reimbursement from a central LRT-operated system. Competing operators would be able to develop their own fare stuctures, while passengers would have one contactless card and drivers would leave it to the machine to check, giving a green light and sound if accepted. Sir Wilfrid had previously been in charge of MTRC, the Hong Kong railway system, where a similar system was being developed. Others within LRT, including David Bayliss, Director of Planning, saw this as a practical way of fulfilling the original Autocheck vision of two stream boarding, allowing extension of one-person bus operation.

WCL, the suppliers of the Underground Ticketing System (UTS), had tested a prototype card with LUL staff at St James's Park Station. This was called the GoCard, though it was particularly thick and we christened it the 'smart brick'. It gave good results, but LUL were extending UTS throughout the Underground and had no need for a new system at that time. Wayfarer, who had now fitted the entire London OPO bus fleet with new ticket machines, were aware of developments and keen to be involved. Thorn EMI were now working with a Finnish company, BusCom, who had developed a contactless system for ski lifts. Users could keep the card within their gloves and just touch their gloved hand to the cardreader each time they took a ride. This had been fitted to buses in Oulu, in the north of Finland, with stored value tickets that had one ride deducted each time the passenger boarded. There were also trials of a different system in Germany, with passengers touching their cards to the reader when boarding and alighting from the bus.

This all looked promising, and I was joined by

Publicity leaflet for the 212 Smartcard trial and a Smartcard wallet.

Beow right: The Buscom equipment on an Olympian of Capital Citybus. Driver John Caygill had been at Walthamstow garage and then moved to work for Capital Citybus when Walthamstow closed. He was enthusiastic about the new system, saying that, "If all the passes were on a Smartcard, and every bus had a cardreader, it would make our job a hundred times easier."

two team members, one technical, the other with analytical and reporting skills. I visited the two small towns in Northern Germany which had experimental systems, but which needed further development, and then to Oulu in March 1992.

The BusCom system was very simple and stylish. A small, eye-catching, cardreader was mounted by the driver. The tickets were coded with 10 rides, and one ride was deducted each time the passenger boarded the bus, with a satisfying 'beep'. Further value could be added to the card at the central enquiry office or at newsagents around the city.

We asked to travel on a rush hour service, and were told to wait at the stop outside our hotel early the next morning to catch the bus on its outward journey so that we could watch boarding on its busy return trip. Now Oulu is north of the Arctic Circle, this was early March, we had just arrived from London, and Finland is two hours ahead of the UK. So the next morning at 06.30 local time, 04.30 London time, we waited in sub-zero temperatures at the bus stop, wearing all the clothes we had with us. Thankfully the bus was on time. The system clearly worked well, and passengers young and old, large and small, fit and less-able, used the system without difficulty. Being Finland in the winter, schoolkids got on carrying skis, and we were fully convinced when another passenger got on with crutches and a leg in plaster - après-ski?

We visited local stores selling the tickets and the company's enquiry office, and we were taken to the ski run where their system was first installed - the first and only time I have used skis! We also visited the design consultancy in Helsinki who had created the BusCom unit, and described themselves as 'experts in the man-machine interface'. Unfortunately, their headquarters building was surrounded by roads which were being remade at the time, with whole areas fenced off, and our guide walked around looking for the entrance, which he eventually found. I observed that these people were experts in the man-machine interface, but we couldn't find the door - a comment which I then spotted being translated to the Managing Director before we were introduced to him! We also visited the BusCom factory to see the units being made and their proposed developments of the system.

The BusCom system was pleasingly simple, but we needed to know that this, and any Smartcard system, would work well with everyday bus passengers and drivers in the demanding London bus environment. It was agreed to borrow a few sets of equipment for a simple trial on one route. In May, we produced a Feasibility Study with a proposal for a demonstration project and, if successful, a full trial. This was approved, and the BEST Project - Bus Electronic Smartcard Ticketing - was born.

We needed a small self-contained route, with dedicated buses and staff, regular passengers and a flat fare. I knew just such a route, the 212 from Walthamstow to Chingford, because I had operated it at Walthamstow and it was now run by Capital Citybus with five single-door Metrobuses and a regular team of drivers, though four Midibuses ran it on Sundays. Leon Daniels, MD of Capital Citybus was very supportive of the idea and gave his full cooperation. Equipment was borrowed from Buscom and fitted to the buses by LRT staff, with technical support from Thorn EMI. I recruited a group of students to approach Old Age Pensioners on the bus to use the cards, while schoolchildren and other regular passengers with Bus Passes were given smartcards. A smaller 'trial within the trial' tested the use of a stored value card.

We ran the system from September to December 1992. The BusCom reader flashed a green light and gave a sound when the smartcard was presented to it. From this, the driver accepted it as a valid pass. It was a simple practical trial and there was no link to the driver's ticket machine. And it was successful - the cards and solid-state bus readers avoided the reliability problems experienced with Autocheck, boarding speeds were good, and staff and passengers were happy. We produced a Feasibility Report based on these results, proposing how the technology could be used and, as a result, funding was approved for a large-scale trial of bus smartcard ticketing, which would take place in Harrow.

The Harrow smartcard trial

This was designed as a full-scale trial of the system in the way in which it might be implemented across London, with cardreaders linked to the driver's ticket machine, smartcards replicating existing types of off-bus tickets, and testing a stored-value ticket. A full tendering process was carried out after discussions with suppliers including Buscom (through Thorn EMI), AES (an Australian company who had acquired Prodata of Belgium), and WCL with Wayfarer. The system installed in Harrow included modified London Wayfarer 2 ticket machines with large capacity drivers' modules, AES Scanpoint readers on 150 buses, WCL readers on 50 buses, and 40,000 GEC smartcards for passenger use.

Harrow was chosen as a relatively self-contained area of the right size for the trial. It was planned to include 200 buses on the 21 routes there. Harrow Weald garage was fully involved, as were London United, Sovereign, Luton & District and BTS on their tendered services. The majority of buses had double-width entrances with two cardreaders, and separate exits; a few had one door and only one reader. At the time, this was the largest contactless smartcard scheme in the world.

Production of the bus equipment proceeded rapidly, but severe delays occurred in GEC providing the cards and this became the critical issue for the project. The result was that Sir Wilfrid Newton sent a brief letter to Sir Arnold Weinstock, Chairman of GEC, explaining the importance of our project and asking him if he would look into the delay. The immediate result was that the Managing Director of GEC Card Technology was replaced by the end of the week. Cards then began to appear, but further problems arose. They were constructed as a 'sandwich' with hard outer layers and inner layers holding the memory chip and radio aerial. It proved easy to push a thumbnail into the middle of this 'sandwich' and pull the card apart - and we knew that some of our passengers would delight in

doing this. We demonstrated this to GEC who were not pleased to see their expensive prototypes in pieces! Eventually, the problem was solved, and testing could commence.

The Harrow trial eventually started in February 1994. Although LUL were not at that time pursuing smartcard technology themselves, they were fully involved and took a great interest in our progress. Local LUL Revenue Protection staff helped supervise the trial and use of the tickets. A public information office was set up in the new Harrow Bus Station, the focal point of local services, to give information and issue smartcards. Equipment was bought to print an instant photograph of the holder on the face of the Smart Photocard, and these were issued to holders of Travelcards and Bus Passes in exchange for their old Photocard. A surplus Leyland National bus was also used as a mobile issuing point, visiting locations in the area around Harrow, but in practice the Harrow Bus Station office was sufficient. Local PASS agents also had cardreaders which were used to renew the tickets on Smart Photocards.

Smart Photocards were also issued to Pensioners, but the quality of the photograph was not good - in black and white with relatively poor definition - and some Pensioners disliked them. We soon realised that the photos on some of their Photocards had been taken many years before, and they were not necessarily happy replacing their familiar photo with one taken that day!

In a second stage of the trial, Farecards were tested from February 1995. These were stored-value cards bought from PASS agents with a set value already on them. On boarding the bus, the passenger told the driver what journey they wanted to make, and the driver used the ticket machine to take the cost off the Farecard and issue a paper ticket. Passengers could also add value to the card on-bus. Take-up of Farecards was not great, and since by then the trial was approaching its end, it was decided to give loaded cards free to staff and to selected groups of passengers in the area, including hospital staff, school teachers and the families of bus drivers. This gave some free travel in exchange for them completing a survey about their experiences using the system.

Some thought was also given to having exit cardreaders which would automatically read every card passing through the exit doorway. However, this was not taken further because the readers would be likely to collect huge volumes of spurious data from everyone passing near the door, even if they had just boarded the bus, or who were travelling near the exit door on a fully loaded vehicle.

The Harrow smartcard reader in use next to the driver's ticket machine.

From July 1995, the National Westminster bank ran a comparable trial of their Mondex cashless card system, choosing Swindon as their typical self-contained small town. We liaised with them and visited each other's trials, but theirs was on a significantly smaller scale, did not gain widespread public acceptance, and was closed after a time.

The Harrow trial ended at Christmas 1995. Around 700 bus drivers and 235 buses of nine different types and five operators had been involved. 20,000 passengers made nearly 5 million journeys, with 10,000 passenger journeys on a typical weekday. Over 5,000 journeys were made with blind persons' Smartcards, and one card was completely chewed up by a dog! Overall, the system worked well - it was reliable, while both staff and passengers were happy to use it. Ticket checking - and so bus boarding - was faster and more accurate, the tickets themselves were more secure, and considerable data was now available on the journeys being made. So the trial was successful and it laid the foundations for a fleetwide system across London's buses, whether they were privatised, deregulated or whatever structure came about. The strong business case included the ability to extend OPO, to reduce fraud due to the security of smartcard systems, to market a wider range of tickets without making the job of the driver more complicated, and in particular to permit travel on any operator's buses with the same ticket, with an accounting system that would record all the journey data to properly allocate the revenues between operators.

LUL now concluded that they should also participate to create a multi-modal contactless system, which later emerged as the PRESTIGE Project and the introduction of the Oyster card. Internationally, smartcard systems were by then developing worldwide, with trial systems in Paris and Japan, some experiments in the USA, a comprehensive system planned in Hong Kong and a very quick implementation in Seoul, South Korea.

Once Oyster Cards became widespread in London, there was a rapid expansion in the use of contactless cards so that most bank cards can now work this way. Transport for London developed the system further so that any UK bank card can be used in place of an Oyster Card, and the almost total use of these cards then enabled TfL to bring cash payment on buses to an end. This caused short term inconvenience to a small number of bus passengers, but the effect on bus operations has been dramatic, with faster boarding, the complete removal of cash from the system, a wider range of tickets becoming possible, and significantly improved management information on the journeys being made, so improving the bus services provided.

Writing this chapter during the Coronavirus lockdown in Spring 2020, it is striking to see the significance that contactless cards have had in letting people pay for goods and services without touching any equipment other than their own card, and without exchanging cash with shop and transport staff. And perhaps it all follows from a ride on a ski lift in Finland in 1992!

My thanks to Andy Griffiths and Paul London for conversations in the preparation of this chapter.

We've got a smarter way to hop on a bus around Harrow.

SMART PHOTOCARD

Leaflet front and interior.

8 OPERATING TENDERED BUS SERVICES
Norman Kemp

Changes in the UK bus market in the 1980s were radical, like the politics of the Thatcher government. The 1985 Transport Act brought de-regulation of the UK's provincial buses, the compulsory transition of the many municipal bus companies into arms-length ownership, and privatisation of NBC – the state-owned National Bus Company. At the same time, the regulated bus market in London was opened to competitive tendering. As the evolution – and the politics – of these structural changes is well documented elsewhere, this piece is intended as a practical account of how this new regime was approached by two very different established bus operators based in the County of Kent.

Maidstone, Kent's county town, is located about 40 miles from central London yet only about a 30-minute drive from the Capital's outer borders – indeed, areas such as Orpington and Bexleyheath still retain, even now, the Kent county name in the postal address from their pre-GLC days. Maidstone Borough Council had operated its own transport department until Autumn 1986, services until then being co-ordinated in agreement with Maidstone & District Motor Services Ltd and The East Kent Road Car Co Ltd – larger neighbouring bus operators which were NBC subsidiaries. In accordance with the new legislation, a stand-alone company, Maidstone Borough Transport (Holdings) Ltd, was formed to take on the Council's bus operations. With an identity devised by Ray Stenning's Best Impressions consultancy in one of its earliest commissions, the new business traded as Boro'line Maidstone.

In this new world as a business in its own right, new income streams were essential for Boro'line if overhead costs previously borne through its status as a Council department were to be met. From the outset, it tightened its grip on the bus market locally in Maidstone but this was never going to be enough. To survive, let alone to prosper, it needed to diversify.

Since the first discussions on the tendering of the London bus market, the potential opportunity was being closely followed in Maidstone – and, no doubt, in the board rooms of bus operators big and small, for the same challenges faced everyone in the industry to a greater or lesser degree. Provided one was properly set up for the opportunity, the revenue from contract payments for running London bus routes was less of a gamble than running local bus services where 'bums on seats' paid the bills.

Thus, extension of the company's activities into London was carefully considered because Maidstone's weaker position, looking to the future, had exercised the minds of the management team there. Bids were prepared for a number of the early opportunities offered, in the knowledge that it would take a while to refine bidding technique and costing before a successful conclusion. A 'cheap and cheerful' approach to bus operation had suited the finances of the home operation and, with price being an important consideration in the London bidding process, it was initially felt that the use of cheaper-to-run lighter-weight vehicles, such as the Bedford/Wadham Stringer midibuses in use with Eastern National on the tendered W9 at Enfield, would be as relevant in, say, Orpington as it had been for a decade in Maidstone; your writer remembers taking a Bedford single-decker bus on a route trial as part of the preparation for the submission of a bid for R1.

Though Maidstone's bids for various routes were unsuccessful over a period of many months, valuable experience was being learnt with every bid submitted, and with LRT being very keen to encourage and involve operators to bid for London work, their feedback on each bid was vitally important. The bidding process, though less cumbersome than it was later to become, was also rather less transparent in those days, but this was not a reflection on the probity of those involved but simply because competitive tendering was at the early stages of its development. There was not the same requirement then for the tendering authority to provide unsuccessful bidders with information on important factors such as the 'winning' price and the numbers of bidders, so it was quite difficult to get a feel for how to win a bid, but, equally, a bid that was too cheap was likely to be turned down by LRT because an over-cheap contract price would almost certainly lead to an operator being unable to properly deliver a contract if wage levels were pitched too low or if bus purchase cost more than had been budgeted. Later in his career, your writer, involved only in the mobilisation phase for a new-start operation where bids had been prepared centrally, discovered – at a late stage of the project's mobilisation – a disastrous flaw in a bid which had been missed by both the bidder and LRT; the bidder had calculated the in-service route mileage only in one direction, not for the return trip, thus basing cost estimates on only about 50% of the miles scheduled to be run, and wiping out any chance of profits.

Of course it wasn't possible for the individual bus operators to dictate to LRT which routes were going to be included in the tender programme. Indeed, just which routes were chosen for tendering always

Boro'line and its predecessors had been an avowedly single-deck bus business for many years, epitomised by the sale of the modern Atlantean fleet in the 1970s and their replacement by light-weight single-deckers. Wheels had therefore turned full circle when double-decks were bought for the Eltham-based routes won under contract from London Transport, who specified the use of double-decks but left the choice of manufacturer to the operator. A standardised fleet of 14 Leyland Olympian buses was expected. Bodywork was by newly-established Optare, which had recently re-opened the Roe bus factory in Leeds after its closure by Leyland. The body shape had evolved from the Park Royal-Roe design of a few years previously. Delivery of the new buses was protracted, however, which caused the operator much embarrassment and eventually led to the order for 14 buses being reduced to 11. Replacements in the form of Scania and Volvo double-decks materialised instead. The Bexleyheath terminal of 132 is the setting for 752, the second bus of the order, pictured when new in April 1988. The neat route number/ via blind was a hand-painted one, created in Boro'line's Armstrong Road workshop in Maidstone. A breakdown in communications at the time of manufacture resulted in the front blind boxes being to London Buses' specification, rather than Boro'line's rather smaller standard. Roadside monitoring of the performance of contracted routes was undertaken in those days, and, to facilitate this, it was a contractual requirement for buses to display a 'running number', shown here as a yellow square on the top of the nearside windscreen.

With the new buses intended for Boro'line's London fleet not delivered, operations started with a number of Leyland Atlanteans hired in, primarily from Kingston upon Hull City Transport Ltd, another 'arms-length' municipal operation. WAG379X, a youthful six years old, typified the Hull contribution. It carried a Roe body, built in the same plant at Crossgates, Leeds which, under new owners Optare, was late in producing the Boro'line Olympians.

seemed to be one of the major mysteries of the process, even after the earliest days, but one has to suspect that where an operator had been identified by LRT as showing an interest, perhaps a suitable route or routes nearby were found for inclusion in a future tranche of tendering. A 'near-miss' for Boro'line had been the 197B (Caterham-Croydon) which would have involved a dead run of 45 to 60 minutes in each direction in the road conditions prevailing then, and although the bid piqued the interest of LRT, ultimately it was not awarded. However, this gave the directors confidence that the pricing and general style of tender bids submitted was beginning to get us near to the playing field and indeed, shortly thereafter, Boro'line was successful with a combined bid for 13 vehicles' worth of work as part of a Bexleyheath area scheme. What had become clear through the feedback process for earlier bids was that the cheap and cheerful approach was not a necessary ingredient for success, and the winning bid for routes 132, 228, 233 and 328 specified new-build double-deck buses.

Operators submitted their sealed bids to LRT's Tendered Bus Unit (TBU) and a significant amount of what is nowadays called 'due diligence' would be undertaken by the TBU when a bid had merited serious consideration, including visits to operators' premises and meetings with the principals in the business, particularly to establish the 'wheres and hows' of service operation. Shortly before any award, the operator would receive a phone call from TBU to ascertain whether the operator was still interested, and prepared to accept any award. With the award announcement, the serious work of mobilisation began, with members of the TBU team keeping a watchful eye on progress to ensure no slip-ups near to launch date – there were plenty of spectators at the feast, willing the newbies to fail so that the incumbent could step back in but, at least in South-East London, the problems were all in the incumbents' camps in 1988.

Lead-in times became longer over the years, but were less than six months for that first award to Boro'line. The first pieces in the jigsaw saw buses

Because delivery of the new Leyland /Optare fleet for the Eltham routes was delayed, alternatives were sought, including 701, one of two similar Scania/Alexander buses hurriedly supplied from dealer stock and amongst very few Kent-registered double-decks that year. The other 12 of the buses sourced were supplied through a Ponders End-based dealer (Arlington) who registered the buses there with London marks. The two Scanias (701/702) were speedy and powerful machines, as was Volvo Citybus/Alexander (764) built to Scottish Bus Group specification. These three 'oddball' but thirsty buses tended to spend their days on route 233 which benefited from use of faster inter-urban roads between Sidcup and Swanley. After a period of below-par performance, the newly-privatised Kentish Bus 'upped its game' in Summer 1988 by introducing five similar buses (numbered 701-705 in the Kentish Bus fleet), displacing older Atlanteans from the arduous LRT service 51 onto less strenuous local bus service work in north-west Kent.

ordered and a suitable operating base found. Local authority connections were harnessed to secure a site at the Bexley Borough transport depot in Crayford, near to the routes. With Boro'line's overall business set to increase in size by over 30%, it was necessary to bring in some management assistance to make sure that the eye was not taken off the ball in the existing core business whilst ensuring that the new operation got all the attention it needed to ensure a successful start. Initial scheduling of drivers' duties was outsourced to Reading Buses, and the contact book of an experienced recently-retired municipal general manager was used in a variety of ways, including sourcing an interim bus fleet when, in a big disappointment, the promised delivery date for the new buses slipped back to post-launch.

At a time when the UK bus manufacturing industry was seriously in the doldrums, as orders for new buses had fallen sharply after provincial deregulation, the order for a fleet of fourteen heavyweight Leyland Olympian double decks, bodied by Roe, should have given a welcome fillip to the UK bus building business. In the event, initial deliveries were delayed past the start date of the contract, taking some of the shine off the contract start, and the full order was never fulfilled because Boro'line decided to source alternative vehicles in order to complete the new bus fleet. In the early years of London bus tendering, the bus-manufacturing industry over-promised far too often and let down a lot of customers with belated deliveries - those who have chronicled bus orders and deliveries in that era would not have been aware of the pain and frustration in the operating companies when older, more expensive buses had to be substituted for promised newer ones.

No bus operation can succeed without its front-line staff of drivers and controllers; an early appointment to Boro'line's London team was a manager who was tasked with finding the 30+ staff needed for the new operation. Staff shortages were one of the features of route tendering in London which caused great angst especially in the early 'pre-TUPE' days – nowadays, 'TUPE' legislation allows staff to move with a contract when the operator changes, but there was no such provision then. Great good fortune here, however, was that the overall Bexleyheath area scheme, of which the Boro'line operation was only a small part, caused massive movements of staff between companies, and the pay rate offered bettered that at other local bus garages so positions were quickly filled. With a choice of experienced good calibre staff available to fill all the positions offered, operations got off to an excellent start even though the bus fleet itself only received its new vehicles in following months, after an acrimonious dispute with the builders over the delays which saw alternatives being sourced instead of the last of the planned buses - not a good advert for the

manufacturing industry which had so craved the order which had been placed to help them at a time of distress. In short, tendering brought many benefits to South-East London bus users with a dedicated small team determined to offer a reliable and friendly service, and worthwhile cost savings to LRT to boot. For Boro'line, the operation was a financial success, and its successful launch and sustained post-launch performance surely gave confidence to LRT that bringing in an out-of-area operator was not a gamble, and probably helped to secure further awards for Boro'line, months after the writer had moved on to pastures new in a business development role at Kentish Bus.

Maidstone was one of the nearest of these arms-length municipals to London but, ultimately, the only one to make the break into gaining tendered bus service contracts from London Regional Transport (LRT). Perhaps this stemmed from Maidstone being smaller (hence more vulnerable) than its fellows, being more hemmed in by large and aggressive competitors – on the face of it, Reading Buses was well placed to access the western edge of London in the Heathrow/Uxbridge areas, and Southend Transport in the areas which saw an Ensign Bus presence in due course, for example, but each of those had a more substantial core business on its home patch, and Southend's X1 London Commuter service, with 60-plus coaches in its heyday, was certainly a substantial diversification from its previous co-ordinated 50-plus local bus operation on the Thames Estuary.

Turning then to the Kentish Bus and Coach Company, this had been created in 1986 from the south-eastern quadrant of the London Country empire, whose established operations were closer to London. Its rebranding from London Country South East was another Best Impressions commission, with a maroon/cream livery supposedly based on the colours of the Colchester Corporation buses which had carried a previous member of the senior management team here to and from school. The company had a large commercial bus operation in north and west Kent in 1988 and a small presence in the London tendered bus market, and had been sold in that year to new owners in one of the final stages of the NBC privatisation process. It was generally felt that the last sales of NBC companies comprised the basket cases, and it was brave of the management team from the successful Northumbria Motor Services Ltd, an earlier NBC privatisation, to take on Kentish Bus just months after it had experienced devastating losses of London work in the same tranche which had seen success for Boro'line.

The new owners needed to source a locally-based senior management team for their new acquisition. The challenge for the writer in his new post was two-fold – to reshape the unprofitable but core local bus business in north-west Kent, operating then from

Swanley, Dunton Green, Northfleet and Dartford bus garages, and to secure replacement work in the more-profitable London tendered bus market, where the pace of tendering, and thus potential opportunities, had begun to increase, and where revenues were more certain. Pooling of group resources provided smaller, more economical buses to work in parts of the Kent operation as well as providing some reasonably modern buses to eke out a few years of front-line service on London routes 96 and 269 from 1991 instead of along the Coast Road between Newcastle and Blyth. The biggest obstacle to necessary change, however, was that the front-line staff had been through a long period of negativity and uncertainty, seemingly with little guidance or information from the previous management team about the challenges of a deregulated and privatised world – that competitors were now allowed to cream off much passenger traffic on the best routes was met with disbelief in the company but no real desire to respond. Executing further change was necessary but very hard to achieve with a workforce who were, at best, suspicious and, at worst, downright hostile, and it was no surprise at all that the management's focus gradually moved to building up new business with LRT in London whilst reducing and reshaping the Kent business to just the least-unprofitable parts.

The author's previous experience of setting up a new and successful operation on a site remote from existing operations thus looked to be an appropriate way forward. Successful bidding saw the Kentish Bus name carried to distinctly un-Kentish destinations on a new fleet of 43 Leyland/Northern Counties double-deck buses used on a large operation based from 1990 at a new site in East London. A partnership with the once-state-owned British Road Services (BRS) had been established some years earlier when BRS – just like much of the bus industry - was trying to diversify to survive, using its substantial portfolio of real estate on former railway–owned land. BRS Temple Mills depot had seen its vehicle workshop rebuilt, and hardstanding created, so that it could service the fleet which Kentish Bus bought to operate LRT routes 22A, 22B and 55 which ran nearby in Hackney, the City and the West End.

A new generation of bus company entrepreneurs had resulted from the NBC privatisations and keeping City financiers happy became part of the game, so when it was discovered that the building occupied by the bank which had funded the Northumbria/Kentish Bus buyouts was passed by the 22A, extra-large Kentish Bus fleetnames appeared both amidships and even on the roof of certain of the buses allocated to that service. The company's General Manager thought that the Kentish Bus fleetname would have looked good on buses on the 214 route in the inner north London suburbs because it served Kentish Town, but a bid for this in 1992 proved to be unsuccessful.

A major setback in 1992 which highlighted the scale of the problems still having to be faced was loss of the important contract for service 51 to London Central. Although this loss came at a time when LRT's own free-standing red bus companies were bidding aggressively to regain lost market share and, indeed, to prepare for expected de-regulation in London, the 51 under Kentish stewardship had suffered from poor

Metrobus of Orpington obtained eight brand-new Mercedes/Reeve Burgess buses to launch MiniMetro at Gravesend. This view was taken in the first week of the operation. The eastern terminal point for both the services (A and B) was at Hever Court. Not only the service buses could be captured on film here, but also the driver's rest bus-cum-standby vehicle. The two routes had been carefully designed to challenge established Kentish Bus routes on its busy cross-Gravesend east-west corridor. The young Metrobus company was fleet of foot, its operations unencumbered with the working practices at Kentish Bus which, by 1988, belonged to a previous, regulated and nationalised, era.

It would be fair to say that Kentish Bus was very late in adapting its working practices to the brave new world of local bus deregulation, and, by 1989, more nimble competitors had already eroded the established incumbent's previous monopoly by providing robust 'challenger' routes - notably Transcity on the Dartford/Swanley corridor, and Mini-Metros and Black Horse Buses in Gravesend. The company's strongest operations had traditionally been those on Thames-side, bordering Greater London to the west. There were few opportunities left for expansion using the traditional 'big' buses - Nationals and Atlanteans - which comprised nearly all the Kentish fleet. New 'parent' Proudmutual had a surplus of smaller buses in its Northumbria fleet and homes for some of these were found in Kent by developing new routes which would have been inaccessible to the traditional fleet, with long-standing requests for better penetration of residential areas in Dartford being met with new route 486, reviving a route number traditional to the area but using different roads. The bold Northumbria livery of the bus depicted is unmistakable, but has been adapted for its new role using vinyls.

reliability despite an infusion of new buses replacing an unreliable second-hand fleet with which operations had originally commenced. The issues here arose primarily from entrenched staff attitudes but also from a failure to retain staff in a volatile recruitment market. It could be argued that the red bus operation in London had lost its way in the 1970s/early 1980s, and brought tendering on itself, in not-dissimilar circumstances, with vehicle shortages and 'Spanish Customs' - outdated working practices - amongst the unionised workforce which seemed to focus on anything but the provision of a regular and reliable bus service.

The various companies which had been established from the break-up of London Country had all gained a significant share of the tendered London bus market around the date of privatisation and it is fair to say that all had a far greater amount of labour dispute and vehicle unreliability than neighbouring ex-NBC companies who became LRT contractors under the tendering regime, let alone the new-starts such as the successful Metrobus, also operating in the heart of the Kentish Bus operating area, who had started with nothing but a common-sense clean-sheet approach to employment and productivity issues.

A notable success, however, for Kentish Bus came from a tendered bus route newly-awarded in 1992.

Operation of the busy route 227 between Bromley, Beckenham, Penge and Crystal Palace was based at Dunton Green near Sevenoaks, one of the inherited London Country garages. Poor ridership in the Sevenoaks area had led to heavy cuts in its traditional commercial bus network, so the garage had plenty of spare capacity to accommodate the twelve buses required for this service, restricted by a low-bridge to single-deck operation. It won 1992's London Regional Passengers Committee top award, which was a remarkable achievement as, prior to that, tendered operations from the legacy garages had lacked sparkle, as evidenced by loss of the contract for the 51, but Dunton Green's young management team instilled enthusiasm in drivers, many of whom were newly recruited to the company. This award gave a much-needed confidence boost to the whole company, and was perhaps the turning point for attitudes in the company.

At a time when the finances of public sector organisations such as LRT were under pressure, an innovative solution was used to source buses for the route from the existing Kentish Bus fleet, which had comprised large numbers of Leyland-National single-deck buses, now showing their age. East Lancashire Coachbuilders, with styling input from Best

Impressions, had developed the Greenway bus which involved a total rebuild of a Leyland-National into a brand-new bus, with a smart appearance and use of a 'green' Gardner engine replacing the smoky Leyland units powering the original vehicle. This concept 'ticked various boxes' including price and green credentials, plus a host of Schedule X features, and the resultant vehicles proved to be very adequate and reliable performers on what was as gruelling a route as any in London.

A further Kentish Bus operation to be established remotely from the one-time core business came in 1993 when the operation of route 19 in Inner London commenced. This was the first Routemaster-operated route to pass to the private sector through the tendering process. It proved to be a huge success, not least as its previous operation under London Buses had not been renowned for its reliability. Much more about route 19, including the story of the difficulty in securing an operating base, was told in the now out-of-print book *Working with Routemasters*, but suffice to say that Location! Location! Location! is the most important lesson ever learnt – in establishing a new London bus operation, one needs to find a site in an appropriate location, close to the route. Costs soar with more distant locations, where staff have to make unproductive 'dead' journeys to reach the route from their base, and 'on the road' mechanical issues take a long time to resolve when fitters are not close at hand.

A salutary tale about the importance of finding the right site comes in the period after the author had left Kentish Bus to further his industry career elsewhere in London. Kentish Bus had won a significant parcel of routes spread across a swathe of South East London, and these commenced in 1994. It selected a base which it inexplicably called 'Lewisham' but which was virtually at Surrey Quays, close to Central London, nowhere near Lewisham and far from routes in the tranche such as 138 and 162 which were focused on Bromley. Reassignment of some of the contracts to operators based at closer locations was a sad but inevitable result after 18 months of unreliability.

Lest the foregoing reads as if one tendering success followed another, the received wisdom amongst those operators submitting bids was that only one out of every 20 bids submitted would prove to be successful, so a huge amount of work proved to be abortive. Preparation of a bid became more time-consuming over the years, not least as consideration of facilities for less-able bus users, listed in Schedule X of the specification, became a major focus of the submission and this required information to be sought from bus builders at the bidding stage about the likely type of bus to be bought for any contract. Second-hand buses were occasionally an appropriate choice for an operator's non-compliant proposal, so the price of a new bus would be used in the compliant proposal with a separate proposal based on use of an older bus with features such as contracting hand rails and step edges retro-fitted to meet the Schedule X requirements.

Routes were generally offered for tenders in batches, advertised to operators through the industry press, and with the 'tender pack' then sent out on request. The specification detailed the route to be followed – this

Kentish Bus B-series Leyland-National YPL 439T had been one of a large fleet of similar vehicles which had been new as SNB 439 to London Country, passing in 1986 to the newly-formed London Country South East company. Repainted in 1987 to the new Kentish Bus livery and now numbered 465, it was used on LRT services 42 and P4 until later selected for refurbishment as a Greenway for use on suburban LRT route 227, and now numbered 435. The Kentish Bus livery was refreshed on these extensively-reworked vehicles to include a green band and fleetname, as a contrast to the original maroon and cream colours with black fleetname. The entire Greenway fleet was later given 'dateless' registration plates, this becoming SIB 1282.

Newly-refurbished RML2410 still gleams when captured by the camera in Chelsea, near journey's end, on 15 May 1993. Kentish Bus operation of LRT service 19 (Finsbury Park/Battersea Bridge) had begun only weeks before. The Kentish Bus livery was complemented on these vehicles by between-decks route-branding, whilst the 'London Buses' radiator badge normally found on refurbished RMLs has been replaced by a TEAM 19 badge. Prior to the start of the contract, ownership of the buses had transferred from London Buses to London Regional Transport, who then sub-leased them to the operating company.

was not for negotiation in any way, shape or form as each route, regardless of operator, remained a part of the overall London bus network. Another taboo was to propose a timetable which scheduled buses or drivers across more than one route, where a delay in one area could 'contaminate' an unrelated service if crews or buses became displaced. The timetable, however, was for bidders to prepare, the specification giving first and last bus times and the minimum frequency to be offered. The existing route timetable was included in the 'pack' of papers sent out and was a useful guide, but a ride on the route being offered, though not mandatory, was often useful as it could expose shortcomings in the current timetable. Routes often proved to have too much running time at quieter times of day, for example in the late evening or early on Saturday mornings, and submission of a more realistic timetable could create just the economy to beat a competitor on price. In order to arrive at the bid price, the operator would need to cost the number of staff required to operate the timetable, and while the bid process required driver pay rates and other terms and conditions to be itemised in the submission, a fully-worked out duty schedule was only required to be submitted to LRT after a bid was accepted.

To complete this tale, the writer's Maidstone past caught up with him during his Kentish years,

when the Boro'line company failed and its basket of London contracts was novated to Kentish Bus. Arguably, the company's failure came about because its Maidstone-based bus and coach operations had become uneconomic, especially after a direct attack on its commercial services by Maidstone & District, its one-time partner in the provision of co-ordinated local bus services. However, after its early success in the Bexleyheath network, it had grown quickly thereafter, not just with a series of LRT contract wins but also when LRT's patience with poor operational performance at the Bexleybus subsidiary of London Buses ran out and routes 422 and 492 were added to Boro'line's portfolio, primarily using hired-in and other elderly buses. The original Boro'line set-up at Crayford had seen its fleet of buses receive such servicing as new buses require being dealt with at Maidstone, but suddenly running Leyland Nationals and Volvo Ailsas from a base without a pit was a different matter altogether and the quality of the whole operation was never the same again, presumably adding to the growing problems faced in Maidstone. The Crayford site, the staff and vehicles continued to be used by Kentish Bus for a while after the contracts transferred across but space was later found to accommodate all the work in the nearby Kentish Bus Dartford garage.

9 DESIGNING LIVERIES FOR LONDON

Ray Stenning

By the time of the creation of the separate London Buses operating companies in preparation for privatisation, the reputation of both me and my company, Best Impressions, was growing in stature and we'd carved out a particular niche for creating rather commanding liveries in the years immediately preceding bus deregulation and into the deregulated era, as well as publicity and marketing.

Some of these liveries were to be seen on the fringes of London, like the stylish rich two-tone green with red London & Country (as we more appropriately renamed the somewhat cumbersome sounding London Country South West) and that for neighbouring Kentish Bus, both around 1986/7. Later we designed an adaptation of the London & Country livery for the company's offshoot for tendered bus work based in Camberwell, Londonlinks.

It was also about this time that London Regional Transport's Tendered Bus Unit headed up by Nick Newton came into being. It's all a bit of a blur now chronologically, but we began designing liveries for some of the 'outside' companies winning tenders to run London bus routes. Len Wright had set up London Buslines in West London in 1985 for that very purpose and when he bought new Northern Counties bodied Volvos we clothed them in a rather smart and arresting bright yellow base livery set off with brown and orange. Then, when Harris, the coach company over in Grays, won routes south of the river around Lewisham and Blackheath, and up into Ilford, we designed a striking blue and lime green contemporary look. For this we also introduced local brands – Lewisham Link and Ilford Link. The flavour and politics of the day was to encourage outsiders and allow them to be proud of who they were, so local liveries were in.

We had already designed a whole new look for the council-owned former municipal bus operator in Maidstone, which we retitled Boro'line, and this was unveiled on deregulation day, 26 October 1986. Boro'line subsequently bid for London contracts big time, although eventually the business overstretched itself and went bust. Before that, I remember telling managing director Alan Price that the brand name we created was portable and instead of Boro'line Maidstone that appeared on the buses in its home town, we could have Boro'line London or Boro'line Greenwich or whatever was appropriate. He was having none of that (municipal pride or stubbornness) and, rather confusing for bus travellers in the capital, its buses kept the incongruous Maidstone name on them.

Perhaps one of the more visible tendered bus route liveries we designed was that for the important route 24 from Pimlico past Westminster, through parts of the West End and north through Camden to the bottom of Hampstead Heath. This, the first Central London route to be won by a non-London Buses operator, was won by Grey-Green and the company came hot-foot to us to do something striking for this route for the brand-new Alexander bodied Volvo D10Ms that were to be used on them.

With a name like Grey-Green the colours suggested themselves rather obviously, but the catalyst that fired them up was a low broad band of bright orange with white pin-striped accents. The orange was quite significant, as Grey-Green had owned a large coach company based in Brixton, the famous Orange Luxury Coaches. West Midlands Travel up in Birmingham rather liked our Grey Green livery and subsequently plagiarised this for its new livery but in different colours, which was confessed to me later by its managing director.

Another high-profile livery we designed for a route passing through the heart of the capital was that for Routemasters to be used on the busy 19. The tender was won by Kentish Bus, who were going to lease the reburbished Routemasters. I well remember going to Doncaster with Norman Kemp from Kentish Bus, Mike Weston from the Tendered Bus Unit and several others to go through the paint instructions for the guys up there working on them. Light colours rarely sit well on a Routemaster but the skill of this bus livery expert made them look rather impressive, with never a hint of 'mutton dressed as lamb', even if that epithet has on occasion been levelled at him! These were the first Routemasters to be used by a non-London company in London.

Not known to be a shrinking violet, I caused a thoroughly enjoyable minor frisson at 55 Broadway earlier, when invited by Malcolm Wren and Andrew Braddock to discuss working on some publicity for the Tendered Bus Unit and was invited into the building's posh restaurant on the top floor. Having arrived there on my motorbike on that occasion, among the lunching sober-suited denizens of that renowned building was this biker with shaved-head, long black beard and attired in an outrageously flamboyant black leather jacket with ten inch fringes, holding every gaze in freeze-frame for a few delicious moments! Lord Ashfield probably turned in his grave but Frank Pick's ghost would have smiled.

For the successful south London orbital 726, previously a Green Line service, we needed to keep London red as the main colour but added white black and grey to differentiate it from the standard London bus. Expresslink was devised to explain exactly what the service was all about.

One interesting project we worked on for the Tendered Bus Unit was a magazine-style brochure to publicise the massive changes that were occurring in and around Wandsworth in 1991. We sought to detail simply, imaginatively and effectively the basic changes in an attractive and engaging style. It became a bit of a template for further similar ones.

Another one was a livery for the former Green Line south orbital 726, now tendered to London Coaches, for which we designed a simple but striking red, black and white scheme and a new name of Expresslink. Another route branding livery project around that time was for Colin Clubb, managing director of London Northern, for the X43 Red Express limited stop variant of the 43.

During the London Buses sell-off period, I think it was quite a coup to be asked initially by five of the bus companies to produce new privatisation identities for them (six if you count Westlink), although one of them, Leaside, decided not to proceed with us after all (although when it became part of Arriva its buses

One that never saw the light of day was our proposal submitted for a special service to the Millennium Dome. Part of the exercise was to look at a more exciting look to the body styling also.

for a few years did end up wearing the so-called 'cow horns' version of our Arriva livery). Those that did were management/employee buyouts London General, London United, Westlink and Metroline, plus London Central (sold to Go-Ahead). Ultimately, Stagecoach-owned Selkent and East London ended up wearing a Best Impressions livery.

The standard London bus livery then was red with a shallow mid-grey skirt and a thin white line between the decks. Each company had small white logos in standard New Johnston italic capitals with a pictogram representing something of significance to their territory or history. Apart from the tweeness of some pictograms, it was perfectly serviceable and quite smart for the day.

For practical and political reasons, most had no desire to change the basic paint application, but wanted a new identity to sit on this as strikingly as possible, although two of them were prepared to make some changes to paint, but still present a largely red London bus.

London General's pictogram was a B-type bus, which managing director Keith Ludeman told me the staff really liked and although he sympathised with my reservations about its appropriateness for a modern progressive bus company, it had to stay. I also thought the 'General' part of the name was too steeped in the past and had rather an Edwardian aura about it. So

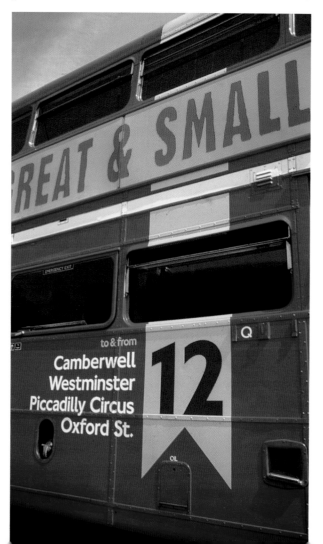

I came up with some designs using the new name of "the London bus" with the visual emphasis on the word London. I knew this would appeal and between us we hoped we could get away with it. Keith took it to 55 Broadway but, alas and not unexpectedly, they wouldn't allow us to get away with such rampant superiority (presumably, it would have been seen as unfair to the other companies).

So London General had to stay, but at least the new logo I designed kept the word London as the prime part of it. The B-type bus was relegated to a much smaller element with the intention of it eventually disappearing, although in the end it never did. We introduced a thin yellow separator between the grey skirt and the main body red. Much later on the company made the grey skirt darker, which I thought improved the livery (wish I'd thought of that!).

I also invented the Streetline name and identity for London General's minibus operations, initially on some Mercedes midibuses, but it looked much more fetching on the sleeker Metroriders. Another project for London General was route branding for the route 11, a fantastic bus route for seeing so many of the capital's sights, even from the rather small windows of a Routemaster!

Keith Ludeman was getting the Leyland Nationals used on Red Arrow services re-engineered by East Lancs into what were called National Greenways, but he objected to the front and rear styling that East Lancs had developed. It was very severe and sorrowful looking. He asked me to see if I could come up with something that retained the concept of a split windscreen with identical panes but had far more 'kerb appeal'. So I did, although some aspects of the design did not quite see the light of day.

For London Central the standard red with grey skirt and thin white mid line livery was kept and my input was to design a new logo. Under London Buses it had adopted a small tea clipper in full sail. So I took that, placed it breaking out of a blue rectangle and made it more dominant and powerful. I also put the visual emphasis on the Central part of name London Central.

I have to admit being most proud of the two route brandings we did on the the Routemasters used on prime routes 12 and 36. This made them really stand out but respected, even enhanced, the familiar lines and profile of the red Routemaster bus.

I recall bumping into London United's managing director David Humphries at the annual Birmingham bus show, and he just said we need to talk about our livery. So a week or two later we did. He was prepared

Our route branding for London Central's 12 and 36 routes included this striking ribbon design to help these buses really stand out without causing conflict with the classic Routemaster architecture. The strong vertical emphasis allowed the destinations to 'hang' neatly off the ribbon but form a coherent communication with the route number.

to go further and we created a rather elegant look for the South West London operator by adding a soft pale grey roof and upper deck window surrounds, and redrawing its crest to make a stronger statement, as with the rest of the logo. It was one of the longest lasting liveries of that early London Buses privatisation era, still there on the ALX400 bodied Tridents on the 94 until they were replaced by Enviro400 hybrids. I'd like to believe that was because the 94 is one of my local bus routes!

For Metroline we also veered further away from the London Buses livery. Here we applied a very rich strong blue to the skirt but engineered that to be quite deep, mostly coming up to the top of the wheelarches. It was stretching the rules a bit but we got away with it and very splendid it looked, too – characterful, purposeful, appropriate and modern. This was further enhanced by the stylish fleetname.

For the Stagecoach owned companies we cleverly adapted the rear upward swoops of orange and blue to sit nicely on a red London bus.

Fast forward to 2019, and Jim Thorpe at Uno in Hertfordshire, like me and many others, was appalled at TfL's recent, clumsy, unattractive and largely ineffective attempts at route branding on buses. He managed to persuade TfL to let us do something smart and stylish on the buses he ran on the Barnet local 383 route that Uno was contracted to run. This extended to internal dressing with continuous coves with helpful route diagrams, interesting stories about things on the route, the story of the operator and customer endorsements. All of this gave the route personality and character and endeared it to the local community. It received many favourable comments and certainly made the route stand out from the rest yet remain a red London bus.

A MINIBUS ERA IN EAST LONDON
Stephen Jolly

I have held 14 jobs in road and rail transport. My sixth job was as development manager for Harry Blundred's minibus expansion plans in the late 1980s. Harry Blundred and fellow National Bus Company (NBC) managers at Devon General, in Exeter, had been the first team to successfully buy a company from the state in the general sale of the NBC fleets into the private sector. When I joined, they had already created a parent company, Transit Holdings. They were competing with the Oxford Bus Company in that city and between there and the Capital. Exciting times in the deregulated bus industry!

The job was based with Transit Holdings. Harry was clear at my interview in November 1987. He wanted new-start operations in the southern counties: "Like a Tesco store in every town but with 40 minibuses. They should run from a yard, with a Portakabin for a controller." His successful model for this was the Green minibus unit in Exeter. The city's big-bus operations had

recently been replaced by red, blue and green minibus fleets, each of 30 Ford Transits and each managed by one controller. Minibuses ran very frequently in the city area. He thought frequency was everything. Patronage had increased, particularly in the evenings.

I was sent to develop schemes in Basingstoke, Luton, Portsmouth and in Gosport and Fareham. Harry continued to run Devon and oversaw expansion plans, aided by Richard Bowler, the former boss of South Midland, a business recently acquired by Transit Holdings. Harry's ex-wife, Janet, ran the Oxford operations. Then, Harry met the chief transport planner of the London Docklands Development Corporation (LDDC), Howard Potter, at a conference. Howard said how unhappy the LDDC was with London Buses. Why didn't Harry start bus operations in Docklands? Howard shared a report with us, 'We've got the trains and boats and planes, 'What about the buses?' by Transportation Planning Associates (TPA).

All maps and artwork for promoting the seven-route operation were produced in Exeter and were similar in style to contemporary publications for the other operations in Oxford and Devon.

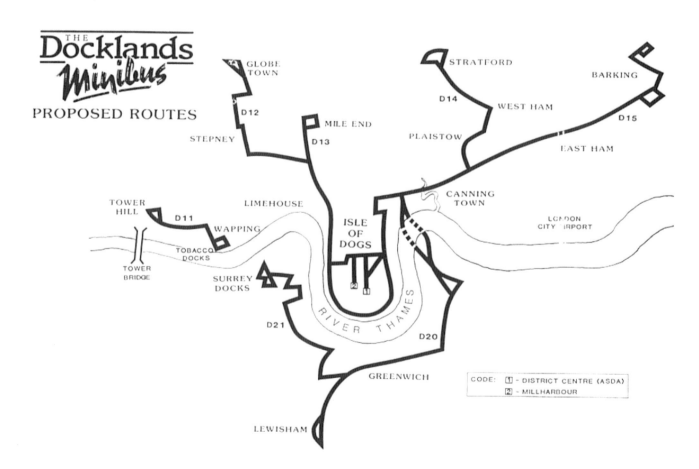

The Docklands Clipper Mile End to the Isle of Dogs Enterprise Zone service was introduced in 1984, three years before the DLR opened. This was operated by branded Leyland Nationals that went through the former West India and Millwall Docks systems, instead of around them like the established 277 bus. As these Nationals seemed to frequently fail, service quality declined as a result. Anecdotally, I cannot recall seeing the advertised service frequency being maintained by non-branded substitutes.

I was sent back to east London, where I had left the Docklands Light Railway at the end of 1987, to plan a 100-minibus fleet to improve bus services to and from the Isle of Dogs. The figure of '100' was more of a political statement rather than being based on an actual planned fleet size.

Few bus improvements had taken place in the area. While it might be thought I would be critical of London Bus operations, they were generally unimpressive with frequent gapping and buses running in pairs. When based in Poplar before the railway opened, the embryonic DLR team used to fill the two Chiswick-supplied staff cars to travel daily to and from Aldgate bus station where the cars were parked overnight, rather than hazard waiting for a bus.

I set about planning the new routes. The TPA consultants had already identified corridors and I adopted their notional route numbers in some cases. I walked the streets, rode on the red buses and subscribed to the LRT bus stop timetable panel service that delivered large quantities of these paper display panels to my home address. I simulated journey times driving cars along my proposed routes. I monitored frequencies and loadings at many bus stops. I recall fearing having minibuses severely delayed south of the Blackwall Tunnel and east of the infamous Canning Town Flyover, and not only at peak times. I drew up summer and winter timetables and after the services started these fears did not become reality.

I had doubts though about a service to distant Barking, which seemed a long way away. I turned the route back just beyond Barking Station at what was a rather unsavoury estate location. Once the route started, drivers soon told me I should have planned the service to run on northwards to Ilford town centre. They were right and when planning later phases I spent a lot of time getting to know something about Ilford's suburbs.

Before the start of the D12 service to Globe Town permission was obtained from Tower Hamlets Council to attach bus stop flags to lamp posts on sections of the route without existing services. An Exeter team put the signs up as shown here, travelling in a decorated minibus. Even before the team returned to the depot that evening, complaints had been received from residents in the houses in the background, fearing not unreasonably that double-deckers would soon be stopping there.

Pictured in the ASDA store car park with a DLR train in the background, Transit 223 displays the large hinged cab door design which caused parking problems in the depot and when exiting a stationary bus on public roads. Just visible is the small black fleet number plate fixed to the lower offside body where a refuelling cap might have been. This was a continuation of a practice of using metal fleet number plates originating many decades before with Western National, then applied to Devon General buses in the NBC era. Transits' refuelling caps were on the nearside however.

The Transport Act 1985 had provided for London Local Services potentially being run by operators other than London Regional Transport (LRT). Although LRT did not object to the 'London Local Services Licence' application we made, a public inquiry was held by the Metropolitan Traffic Commissioner. Seven route licences were granted that included the desired Hail and Ride sections. This became the first big new-start bus operation since the previous generation of bus operators had been absorbed by the London Passenger Transport Board in the 1930s.

LRT was not required to include the operation in the revenue-sharing Travelcard scheme. At the time and subsequently, this was regarded as a major drawback for the new operation's revenue flow. There would have very likely been extended arguments about apportionment settlements if the operation had been included. Payment would in any case have been retrospective.

There was no doubt what type of bus we would use from the newly-acquired garage at Silvertown in the former Royal Docks: Mellor-bodied Ford Transits. This body was a development of the earlier so-called 'Bread van' type. It had been designed by Devon General's engineering director, Clifford Webb, an ex-Leyland man. A man of relatively few words, he told me that he designed the body for standing passengers, reasoning

if they were comfortable enough, all should be well for the seated ones.

One drawback was the cumbersome cab sliding door. On some batches this was replaced with an equally massive full-height hinged door which caused its own problems when parking and when getting out of the bus when stationary on public roads. The door was bigger than those used on half-cab double-deckers. It was an attractive design overall though and disguised the Ford van underpinnings.

The blue, red and white bus livery had been designed in Exeter and was a shameless copy of the DLR train livery. It came as a surprise to me when first I saw it. Harry was evidently impressed with the DLR image.

As with many body designs, the devil resided in the detail. There were sharp edges around the back of the destination box; I have scars to prove it. The rear emergency door fitted over the edge of the rear body panels, not in between them, causing problems. It was proud of the rear end. The fragile warning latch inside was not tough enough, frequently setting off the cab buzzer, in theory rending the bus unfit for public service until replaced. In the Oxford operation, drivers of competing full-sized buses were known to come up behind the Transits, giving them a little nudge to knock the emergency door, so pushing the latch on the lock off its mountings.

Finding an operating centre in the Isle of Dogs was difficult. Space was needed for parking, for drivers to take their statutory breaks and for somewhere to pick up passengers. Space was available in the car park at the only new supermarket, an ASDA store near the former Millwall Docks. We were reliant on the goodwill of the local manager, a person I had met in my previous DLR job. He gave us free parking, bus stop access, café and toilets in return for some free shoppers' bus routes run towards Globe Town before the D12 service launch.

Our driver conduct on the road was something I worried about before the launch but we had few issues to deal with. London Buses drivers were well behaved towards us except on the Isle of Dogs. There, I and other drivers sometimes found ourselves 'bracketed' between two double-deckers from stop to stop all the way to Mile End.

At Mile End I had planned the route to loop past the actual station entrance using side streets, something only a small bus could do. To this day, rail-bus interchange between Burdett Road bus stops and the station remains very poor.

A feature of the group's scheduling of minibus operations that I liked was the practice of the driver keeping his/her bus during meal breaks. This avoided driver changes on the road with passengers sometimes being left stranded awaiting the next driver. Driver changes at the Queen's Lane stop in High Street were and still are a feature of Oxford Bus Company's operations. Harry recalled the disadvantages for passengers from the time when he had worked there. In scheduling terms, as soon as the Peak Vehicle Requirement could be reduced after 09:00hrs, the driver with his/her bus who started first that morning 'Came out of the timetable,' followed by all other drivers in rotation. Such attention to detail was an example of the more passenger-focused attitude of bus managers to customers. I still find when reading some enthusiasts' publications that the package of passenger benefits brought by or reintroduced by minibuses is overlooked or disregarded. Without the ASDA base, and the remote Silvertown depot, driver changes would have been difficult as it was for the Oxford fleet, the depot there being beyond the ring road.

Being excluded from Travelcard, it was logical to use provincial ticketing methods though the orange-coloured seven days free travel ticket would have been a generous offer. The yellow weekly pass was not meant to be transferable but Harry was relaxed about it being shared within a family or between individuals as it could only ever be used by one person at a time. The launch brochure was an attempt at identifying with potential audiences even though the outcome would today be regarded as suggesting some rather crude stereotyping.

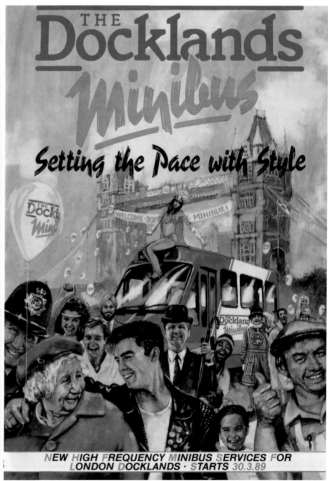

A benefit for the minibus operator was the dramatically reduced need to hold spare parts. Here as with other group operations, the local Ford dealer held parts as 'Imprest stock' on our behalf against possible future needs: a different situation to parts stocking to keep Leyland Nationals or Bristol VRTs on the road at the time.

Although Harry's operations were often regarded as swash-buckling affairs, and Harry enjoyed a reputation for being a bold entrepreneur, financial control by his Exeter team was in practice orthodox and tight. Financial projection tables looked as far forward as 1997. Docklands was seen as a longer-term investment by his finance director. The depot in Silvertown was bought as a freehold investment, contrary to the earlier wish to rent open yards in the provinces.

The revenue build-up was slow although we had one quick win with the takings from the Isle of Dogs to Mile End Station service. Soon the average cash amount taken per driver on Saturdays matched the £93 average per driver/shift returns in the Exeter Green minibus unit. This service met the needs of the existing residents - not new office workers - who lived in a U-shaped settlement strip with the river on one side and the old dock walls on the other, which Harry likened to running a seafront service in a seaside town.

Once the licences were granted the pressure was on to start the routes. We advertised for drivers who were interviewed in the Plaistow Job Centre where we were made welcome until the manager saw the size of the phone bill we had run up and we were summarily ejected. There was a business suite in the new London City Airport though.

The biggest problem was not in finding suitable applicants but in getting PSV test slots for them. We hosted Exeter driver-training staff who would take three test applicants away for the day, frequently having to travel as far as places like Nottingham where there were test appointments available. Days when up to three 'fails' were recorded were fortunately not that frequent.

Having been awarded the licences after the Commissioner's hearing, the first routes, D11, Wapping and The Tower and D13, to Mile End Station, started in March 1989 and were followed by others at intervals thereafter. Because of the shortage of drivers, services did not start at the planned high frequencies nor generally cover the whole traffic day from start to finish. The D12 Globe Town service was launched by Michael Portillo MP, then Minister of Public Transport on 7th July. This served one of the areas where, after much street-walking, I had discovered big gaps in the London Buses network coverage.

I divided my time between driving in Docklands and planning work. I was not beyond Harry's reach as he had supplied with me an early mobile phone with the

While Transit Holdings normally used colour for timetable publicity, it was not perhaps used to great effect on the individual Docklands route leaflets. The essential travel information was rather lost at the bottom of the leaflet.

necessary large brick battery to carry around. Actually, the equivalent of several bricks. Once he called me when I was supposed to be planning routes in Gosport but was about to enter HMS *Alliance*, the preserved submarine based there.

My draft timetables were perused in great detail when I sent them by facsimile transmission to Exeter. When planning the D14 Stratford route, I had set one of the timing points outside the East London Cemetery and I could not resist changing it to 'Cemetery Gates,' in memory of Reg Varney of 'On the Buses' fame. Lavender Hill Cemetery gates was the location used, I believe, in the tv series. I sent off the draft timetable. Within a few hours Harry called. I was reprimanded for not taking the job seriously. No detail escaped him.

I also developed several Stage 2, or Plan B, schemes for greater east London which I still have. In our original written response to the consultants' report we had scoped out far more routes than we sought licences for at that stage. I further refined my thoughts after seeing the little Transits looking lost among bigger Routemasters at East Ham. They had little street presence, particularly as services were launched at lower frequencies than planned, due to the driver shortages.

I planned future growth based on pairs of routes sharing a common section, to be launched at the same time to give better combined frequencies over their common sections. As I had found in Tower Hamlets, so I also found around Ilford; there were large areas of mature residential districts without bus services. Former bus routes leave no record on the streets of their existence but several Docklands routes filled gaps in the London network.

For career reasons I moved back into railway projects offering better longer-term employment prospects. I joined the new Jubilee Line Extension Parliamentary Team later in 1989. I did not engage with buses again until helping to plan the Cambridgeshire Guided Busway earlier in the present century.

As recorded elsewhere, the original Docklands operation closed in November 1990. A contract operation for Reuters staff continued, Reuters having approached me about such an operation. This smaller business was run by Frank Cheroomi, a driver I had appointed. He made an enduring success of it. Transit Holdings returned quickly to London in March 1993 but this time running LRT contracts in the Barking area. Many of the blue minibuses became 'Blue Admiral' minibuses when transferred to the group's new Portsmouth operations. Although none are believed to have survived into preservation, one of the very similar Oxford Ford Transits was later restored by Stagecoach and donated to the Oxford Bus Museum.

Several such schemes, pairing or grouping future routes together, were drafted for consideration by the author. The Stratford and East Ham area routes would have been easier to operate from the Silvertown depot and involved less dead mileage than running the original Isle of Dogs routes.

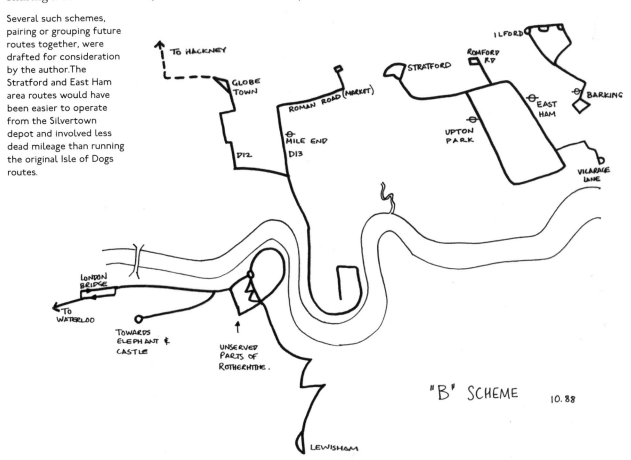

TO HACKNEY
GLOBE TOWN
ROMAN ROAD (MARKET)
MILE END
D12
D13
STRATFORD
ROMFORD RD
ILFORD
EAST HAM
BARKING
UPTON PARK
VICARAGE LANE
LONDON BRIDGE
TO WATERLOO
TOWARDS ELEPHANT & CASTLE
UNSERVED PARTS OF ROTHERHITHE.
LEWISHAM
"B" SCHEME   10.88

11 BUS BLINDS: MANUFACTURE
Malcolm Randles

Ever since rigid destination board displays stopped being practical to use by bus operators, the most convenient and easiest method of having available as many displays as possible was to use a simple roller blind. The process used to get the names onto the roller blind was, and still is, screen process printing.

Screen printing is a very simple process whereby the blind material is placed on a base/table and then a frame with a stencil of the artwork applied on the mesh is lowered down onto the material, which then has ink pushed through this mesh transferring the image onto the material below.

The method of getting the artwork onto the mesh has changed a few times over the years. Originally we used hand-cut paper lettering that after a lengthy process of building up numerous letter size alphabets had to be manually spaced, spelling the word onto a tissue paper which transferred onto the silk mesh when ink was pulled over it. This method had many faults which included incorrect spelling of the destinations, inconsistent displaying of the same names and more frequently letters remaining stuck to the material and

thereby missing from the next and subsequent blinds until spotted by one of the printers or carriers, of whom I will explain more later on. Next came ironed or stuck on stencils which were better in that they very rarely came off, but the process of hand cutting was still required and therefore still a very long winded method in getting a stencil onto a screen.

In the early to mid-1980s various different photographic methods were used, some of which required the setting of each display on a Typositor machine in miniature and then being blown up to full size in a light restricted darkroom on an enlarger onto lithographic film; this was then developed in a wet film processor and when dried, transferred to the screens which had been coated in a light sensitive emulsion before being washed out with a pressurised water gun. A similar emulsion is still used today, although from 1990 onwards computers installed with design and letter programs have been the preferred way to set each display before the stencil is cut out full size on an attached vinyl cutting machine known as a plotter. The advantages of this method are many, mainly due

Inside the Boards and Blinds shop at Chiswick works about 1930. From the production of the first blinds here in the latter half of the 1920s up to the mid-1980s, production was by means of silk screen printed paper labels being applied to rolls of muslin fabric.

Three photos taken at Aldenham works in 1977 showing stages of destination blind production. Pre-cut paper letters are being laid out ready for the silk screen to be lowered onto them and having black ink applied.

to the fact that the stencil is cut full size and is not being enlarged from a miniature thereby improving the final image quality immensely, also no chemicals or darkroom are required making this process much more friendly for the environment.

The method of drying each print run has also changed over the years, from originally being hung over rods which were fitted from the factory ceiling to air dry in a natural way. This process, although quite cost effective, was slow and time consuming; it also created very strong aromas off the oil based inks that were used at the time. Eventually and inevitably this method was replaced by placing the wet blind on a conveyer belt which passed through a heater dryer and cooler which dried the print run straightaway. The heater drier method was a great step forward as it enabled the blinds to be reprinted far more quickly and also reduced each printing team from four to just three persons.

When the blinds had to be air dried, which was also during the period when paper lettering was still being used, a team would consist of two printers, one hanger and one carrier. The printer's job was to print the blinds and the hanger's job was to climb the ladder and hang the blind to dry. The carrier's job was very important because as well as carrying the blind behind the hanger he had to check each destination to make sure that no letters had moved, and more importantly that none had come off and remained stuck to the blind.

When the heater drier system was introduced a team of just three people could carry out the process: two printers and a third person who would be sat at the end of the conveyor belt rolling the dry blind ready for the next printing process. His responsibility was also to check the blind was dry and when paper lettering was still in use he also had to do the job of a carrier and check that no letters had moved or had remained stuck to the blind. Of course his job became a little easier when the stencil was stuck to the screen and therefore did not move or come off.

Today we still screen print a destination blind in exactly the same way we have always done, on a manual screen printing table with a manual squeegee arm which is used to force the ink, now water based, through the mesh to produce a finished blind, although the material we use is no longer linen and is either Tyvek or Polyester. Tyvek was introduced in 1975 and is made from a very strong spun-bonded polyethylene fibre that feels very much like paper. Although being very light in weight it was very difficult to tear and, though it let water vapour pass through it, would not allow liquid water to penetrate, making it ideal for destination blind use. Polyester, which itself replaced PVC material in the early 1980s, is now the preferred choice for all modern day coded electronically operated destination blinds, mainly due to the very high translucent quality offered by the ultrathin 50 micron finished material.

The introduction of SMARTBLIND by McKenna Brothers greatly improved the clarity and legibility of the displays by using a sealed enclosed unit to display the printed blind with a direct light source, originally a fluorescent tube and latterly and currently LEDs perfectly positioned central to the set of motorised rollers. All blinds are printed with a continuous clock and data track along one edge which, when fitted in the unit, passes through a sensor which accurately positions the blind for optimum readability. This very intelligent system also makes the driver's job of changing between route and destination far easier than the original method of using a hand-wind controller, especially when going from end to end on a lengthy

Left: An example of one of the early dot matrix displays tried out on a small number of buses in London in the late 1980s.

Right: A panel from 2011 during the period, from the mid-1990s, when blinds were yellow on black. From 2012 a reversion to white on black began.

blind. A simple push-button controller is positioned inside the driver's cab from which he can change all four blind displays on the front, side and rear of his vehicle simultaneously. This controller can also operate any on-board audio/visual information signs, like route details and next stop indication information, making the whole product and system more helpful.

During the 1980s some operators chose to trial, then use, a new technology which made use of a black board consisting of coated yellow flip dots. To form each character, by use of an electronically controlled pin the yellow dots would flip to become black or remain forward facing to ultimately create and display the destination required. These systems were convenient to use but not very customer friendly as they frequently produced a scrambled egg effect making the destination totally unreadable for any intending passenger. Even when correctly functioning and displayed, because the signs were front lit, the end results were very difficult to read by older people. Many intending passengers with poor or partial sight would often miss their bus and wait for one with a printed blind which they could read much more clearly.

Flip dots were eventually replaced by a much improved technology which used LED lights to form each character; this method was far more reliable than flip dots although the early signs were still difficult to read in varying light conditions by the older generation and people who were partially sighted. The current and latest LED signs have improved tremendously from these early signs with each board having more LEDs which are pitched much closer together, thereby enabling each character to be created very accurately, making the end display much easier for all ages and abilities to read. LED signs have been produced in many colour options, originally in orange and latterly in traditional white with some bus operators even choosing a full colour option.

The names today are created by computer, using the relevant variants of Johnston letterforms. A light box frame is seen here. When the lid is closed onto both a screen coated in a light-sensitive emulsion and the computer-cut stencil, a vacuum is applied, bringing the coated screen and stencil into contact with each other. After a timed exposure, the screen is water washed, creating the image ready for the printing process.

In this image, bus enthusiast Boris Johnson is a willing helper in using a 'weeding' knife to extract the computer-cut lettering to help create the finished stencil ready for the next stage of the process.

Barbican
Finsbury Park 4

Other electronic sign options have been tried and tested over time, like LCD displays which were very heavy, poor in legibility, unreliable in service and very expensive to produce. More recently digital e-ink signs have appeared, similar to the e-reader type device that can store unlimited quantities of literature and digital format magazines, etc. These may yet still prove to be a way forward, although early trials seem to suggest there are some performance differences between a small handheld e-reader and a full bus-size destination display.

The creation on request from Transport for London by Doug Rose, a respected expert on typography and all things relating to graphics and design, of a new set of digital Johnston, the lettering used throughout London Transport since commissioned in 1913 by Frank Pick and finalised in 1916 by Edward Johnston, has made it possible for the latest white LED signs to be trialled on London's buses. These signs have the closest pitch yet

between LEDs, making their readability very similar to that of a traditionally printed destination blind. This, along with the ability of these signs to carry an unlimited number of destination names, allows for much more flexibility; for example when an engineer has to move any number of vehicles from garage to garage without the need for lengthy and potentially costly overnight blind changes. New destinations, if required, can be added literally in seconds without the need to remove any blind to manually cut and splice in new inserts, saving time and cost for the operator, another benefit.

Original purchase and ongoing operating cost, along with the practicality and functionality of any destination sign, will help to determine the display of choice for the future but nothing highlights the true history and heritage of a red London bus more than a traditionally screen printed white-on-black back-lit destination blind.

The polyester is seen here on the inking table, with the stencils above it and the silk screen mesh over that. A viscous ink has been poured across the surface and a transverse squeegee is being pulled along the table. The lettering, in positive form, protects the blind from receiving any ink, acting as a mask. The ink is forced through the silk screen onto the polyester substrate and then the printed blind will be removed for drying.

The finished displays. This photograph was taken during the period (from the mid-1990s) when yellow lettering was specified for use on London bus blinds. In 2012 they began to revert to white.

12 BUS BLINDS: CONTENT
Doug Rose

As referred to by Malcolm Randles, in 2015 I was asked by Leon Daniels, then Managing Director Surface Transport at TfL, to create a library of all blind requirements for McKenna Brothers. This piece explains why the need arose and what happened next.

Blinds production before computers

As Malcolm Randles has explained, individual letters, skilfully hand spaced, used to be cut from paper and were then carefully laid out for silk screen printing. This process was carried out latterly at London Transport's bespoke in-house facility at Aldenham Works. As part of government intervention in the late 1960s, LT's bus design and build was disrupted; by the 1980s all operation was privatized and the extensive overhaul works at Aldenham closed.

By the 1970s 'filmsetting' had become a reality. The earliest machines worked using a negative with consecutive individual alphabet characters in a line. The operator would use a mechanism and 'type' the required character. The machine would spool to this and fire a light beam through it to expose the film behind it. Letter by letter, the film would be exposed and the required destination, via point, or route number, be created. The film artwork was then developed and used as in the silk screen process similar to that described in the Malcolm's piece.

By the time McKenna's took over the production of bus blinds, technology had moved on again and PCs running MSDOS (MicroSoft Disk Operating System and pre 'Windows') were just about capable of simple typesetting tasks. The problem was that LT's Johnston typeface was not commercially available and did not exist in any digital form — neither did the specially-designed 'bus board' condensed variant. Both were available though as film founts (to use the correct spelling) from the filmsetting system. From those film spools, Johnston ('medium' in today's parlance) and bus board condensed were digitized.

The primary restriction of the DOS-based technology was that there was no capability to save any layout typed. If a destination was required unchanged at a later date, it would have to be created again, as if it had not existed before.

Time for something more versatile

During 2009 I had become aware that the excellently printed blinds from McKenna's were causing them problems typographically. Typically, a name set in condensed was a little over half the width of medium, but there was nothing in between the two. I decided to create three levels of condensed. By happenchance Sir Peter Hendy CBE (then Commissioner at TfL) and Leon Daniels became aware of what I was doing and Leon asked me to solve two problems for them: using the most appropriate of my four variations (including the medium) re-create all destinations to optimum spacing and thus legibility; having digitized all four variants with modern software, create an infinitely re-usable library for Mckenna's. The former would result in much clearer displays and the latter would save McKenna's huge amounts of time.

At the outset Leon asked me to ensure that all displays were clear, unambiguous and aesthetically pleasing — and aesthetics play an important role in legibility. Typography is a huge and misunderstood subject and therefore one I can only skirt over in the space available here; I hope however there is sufficient to make clear the importance of the usability of destination displays.

Context is everything

Context is everything in design and all the illustrations on these pages are hopelessly out of context, as are any comparative tests done by parking two buses side-by-side and photographing them from any distance. There are so many variables to consider, some of which are: lighting, weather conditions, vertical viewing angle, horizontal viewing angle, variable viewing distance — and I doubt anyone has typical eyesight anyway, whatever that might mean.

Location, location, location is the immutable maxim of the retail world; in the world of legibility and typography it is: spacing, spacing, spacing. All type-faces work at their best when spaced optimally, and this next point is routinely misunderstood: visually even spaces between adjacent letters is crucial, as is appropriate leading (line spacing).

My personal reason for believing most people don't understand this importance is that humans are amazingly good at reading very poor typesetting, riddled with spelling mistakes and badly spaced. This is because we recognise words by their shapes and the sequence of them making sense to us (this isn't entirely true but will do for now).

The major flaw in this though is that it only works when readers are familiar with the words in front of them; when we are not familiar with them, perhaps in a scientific work, or signs to places we may not know, this ability collapses. Type on signs is not the same as type on a page, though the latter provides other challenges also routinely not understood.

Edward Johnston's work is rightly well respected but I fear often today because of that dreadful word 'heritage'. His letterforms should be revered because of how wonderfully well they fitted the brief and not because he did it a hundred years ago, with resulting 'icon' status attributed that is I feel disrespectful to their true worth. Current bus blinds were still using variants of Johnston, so why had it all gone wrong?

I always work to the principle of 'the four Ds': Discover, Define, Design, Deliver. So many design projects start with the Design, but without having done the investigation (Discover) and establishing the perceived problem (Define) in the first place. Design approaches such as this succeed only by good fortune.

When I was asked to advise a way forward on replacing London's blind displays I have to confess to already having been doing a lot of the 'Discover' bit for the last 50 years, having had a long-term interest in the subject going back to the trolleybus replacement programme. However, the aspect that I did need to investigate was: what was the cause of the degradation that has happened in recent years.

Well to be blunt I believe the problem stems from two quite independent sources. You'll have to wait a bit longer to find out the second one, but the first is the Disability Discrimination Act (DDA), or more specifically from it, the guidelines on route number and destination displays, where in extracts relevant to us it states:

- Characters of not less than 125mm in height [Doug Rose: they mean the capitals but don't say so] when fitted to the front of a vehicle and not less than 70mm in height when fitted to the side of a vehicle;
- Lower case lettering in Helvetica, Arial and other sans serif fonts are easiest to read;
- It is important that ascenders and descenders are not squashed since this will make shape recognition more difficult.

The first point has led to the slavish adherence to height whereas width is not even mentioned. I repeat: spacing, spacing, spacing. Point three warns against squashing descenders (the part of lower case letterforms descending below the baseline, as in 'y' or 'g' etc) and ascenders (the part of letterforms ascending the 'x-height' of a typeface, as in 'b' or 'd' etc). This squashing refers to height, however, they make no mention of the huge degradation in legibility caused by squashing width — and this does far more damage. This particular recommendation refers to dot matrix indicators, more of which later.

The two suggested sans serif typefaces are in my view appalling for legibility but you will have to visit my website to find out my reasoning on this: www.dougrose.co.uk/index_helvetica.htm

The current displays were indeed not squashing the letterforms vertically. However, when a name didn't fit, the inter-letter spacing was being reduced, sometimes dramatically. When this didn't solve the problem the letterforms were squashed and so compounding the problem. My local 263 bus route looked like it went to 'Highbury Bam'. The DDA guidelines were being entirely met and thus demonstrating their short-comings. So that was 'Define' done now too.

The design of every typeface includes the spaces before and after each character, and are not there to be compromised optionally. This is seldom appreciated nowadays as Macs or PCs are used by almost everyone, albeit by few with typographic understanding. McKenna's and their superbly printed blinds were being backed into a corner. Reducing letter spacing reduces legibility. I now need to move back in time.

The design of every typeface includes the spaces before and after each character, which are not there to be compromised optionally. This is seldom appreciated nowadays as Macs or PCs are used by almost everyone, albeit by few with typographic understanding. McKenna's and their superbly printed blinds were being backed into a corner. Reducing letter spacing reduces legibility. I now need to move back in time.

See what I mean?

Understanding Johnston's principles

In 2009 I visited the Victoria & Albert Museum to look at and understand some of Edward Johnston's design sketches that resided there. I was designing a slightly condensed Johnston variant at that time to use on navigation buttons on my website and will refer to this now simply as 'Condensed'.

The successful design of a typeface is the ultimate graphic design contradiction. Each of the individual characters must conform to an overall 'family feel', with each having visually similar stroke thicknesses, general style and proportions, whilst, paradoxically, each must be instantly recognisably different. Edward Johnston was not a type designer but understood this paradox and this is why each of his letterforms are so much more successful than those of any other sans serif face you may wish to consider in this application.

III Gill Sans
III Helvetica
III Univers
IlL Johnston

People sometimes muse at the Johnston 'hockey stick' lower case 'l' but it was designed that way to ensure sufficient letter spacing followed it. In only one of these four sans serif type-faces is it obvious what the word is.

Knowing I had already designed a condensed variant that adhered as faithfully as possible to Edward Johnston's sound principles, and that I had already started designing further variants, born out of all this came the discussion with Leon and Sir Peter Hendy. In my experience these are two very untypical high-ranking officers who have a sensitivity to typography and the vital role the humble bus blind plays in being the entry point to the system and the starting point of every bus journey — all six-and-a-half million a day.

I expect some of you are wondering why there was a need to squash Johnston Medium when a condensed was available. Well I believe the answer is that the often so-called 'bus blind condensed' was too condensed for many names.

By 1939, and based on Edward Johnston's bus board condensed, Harry Carter had designed a more suitable version (Justin Howes, *Johnston's Underground Type*, Capital Transport, 2000). Even this variant was struggling because it could be unnecessarily too condensed and there was nothing between it and Medium available. Herein lies the second problem referred to earlier.

Display boxes fit for purpose

There are three solutions to respecting letter spacing: move away from Johnston (not permitted by LT and now TfL); have a wider blind box (not available); use smaller lettering (not permitted by DDA). This left McKenna's up a blind alley so as to speak. What was needed was a range of Johnston types of varying widths.

So as to create these I had inspected some destination boards from the pre-blind era which of course had hand-cut letters and so there was no standard shape for any letter and each was truly unique. It quickly became clear that in this digital age standardization was needed and instead of one 'bus blind condensed' two were needed in addition to my Condensed. I ended up calling these Extra Condensed and Ultra Condensed.

The effectiveness of Johnston's original designs is in my view unassailable and the only option was to retain his principles but alter the widths of each character, while maintaining those magnificent proportions and their ability to be spaced correctly. Having done that and I hope made it suit the job, I have to say that I don't much like my Condensed as it lacks the purity and elegance of the original — but all design has to embrace compromise and the need dictated the outcome.

Production of the McKenna's library ('Deliver') started in 2015 using a range of condensed typefaces more suited to the job. Of course what is really needed are blind boxes fit for purpose — the right size for the job of displaying the content clearly, and at an appropriate size — rather than making the type fit the space available. Few people buy a picture frame and then try to find a picture that will fit it exactly.

The black boxes represent the actual blind area though the red boxes show the maximum visual area within which the number must fit. It can be seen that Medium and Condensed don't fit for this not particularly difficult number; most 2-digit numbers fit though '44' will not. The truth is that very few of London's route numbers can be displayed to their full effectiveness.

A device re-introduced from paper letter days has been 'superior' 'small caps'. A small cap is about the same height as a lower case 'x' but crucially has the same visual stroke thickness as the lower case. Simply reducing the point size results in thinner characters. The purpose of this device is that being both smaller and top aligned, it arrests and concentrates reader attention and highlights it is different. The existing 4-character 'N205' is difficult to read unless close up.

N31 Swiss Cottage

From top to bottom are: Johnston DR Medium, DR Condensed, DR Extra Condensed and DR Ultra Condensed. Note that the space saving of the three condensed variants is different according to the letters occurring in each word.

Hammersmith
Hammersmith
Hammersmith
Hammersmith

Wimbledon Broadway
Wimbledon Broadway
Wimbledon Broadway
Wimbledon Broadway

Examples

Typographic balance of letterform thickness and sizes is an important aspect of legibility. Here are a few examples of layouts regarded as DDA compliant and the improved type usages for clarity. Some of these examples may not seem important, but the whole point is they should not be obvious. If they were not done the legibility would be reduced.

Angel Road Superstores

The helpfulness of some destination descriptions was questionable and the prevailing route 341 'Angel Road, Superstores' was drawn to my attention by Leon Daniels as these buses also served Angel Islington. When asked to change it to the more appropriate 'Northumberland Park, Angel Road Superstores', it was obviously not going to fit on one line - another DDA recommendation.

Northumberland Park
ANGEL ROAD SUPERSTORES

Northumberland Park
Angel Road Superstores

The qualifier 'Angel Road Superstores' in capitals was in our view a clear winner, though both examples use Condensed. Getting the balance of type height was critical and any bigger and it would fight for too much attention over the primary 'Northumberland Park'. Typographic balance is an important aspect of legibility.

Potters Bar Cranborne Road Industrial Estate

Potters Bar
CRANBORNE ROAD INDUSTRIAL ESTATE

It is often said 'Upper & lower case is easier to read' – but in what circumstances? 'Cranborne Road Industrial Estate' was hugely compromised on existing blinds, as were many others.

The DDA regulations stipulate a minimum cap height of 125mm for front destinations, with 150mm preferred. The new Condensed has made 150mm possible on many names, where previously Medium needed heavy squashing. Side blinds must have a minimum of 70mm cap height. With the range of four Johnston variants available, and the introduction of qualifiers in caps, many were made larger, though several needed subtle visual adjustment for best effect.

Sudbury Town

The majority of reading errors are made when in a hurry and this is another reason why optimum letter spacing and word spacing matter so much. On this front blind 'Sudbury Town' won't fit in Medium and so Condensed has been used. However, a standard word space would look much too wide, owing to the juxtaposed shapes of the 'y' and 'T', so it has been closed up.

Leyton BAKER'S ARMS

Short primary names accompanied by short qualifiers can look better side-by-side. That said, I have thus far avoided them on side blinds as the qualifier would be farther from the door than if below the primary.

St. Paul's

A full stop followed by a word space would look far too wide and so it has been significantly narrowed; less so, but still necessary, a little letter spacing has been removed (this is what 'kerning' actually means and not also the increasing of space) either side of the apostrophe. The intention is that 'fix' helps but goes un-noticed.

31 Kilburn High Road Station

328 Kilburn High Road Stn.

And abbreviations are fine where necessary and obvious.

168 Old Kent Road
TESCO

None of these visual adjustments should show of course, that's the whole point. In this 168 side blind, the subsidiary is visually centred below 'Kent' and not the overall name.

277 Hackney
TOWN HALL

277 Hackney
TOWN HALL

In both examples of this side blind the primary name has been increased and in doing this it of course also gets wider. This allows the lower case 'y' to encroach the vertical space (leading) of the qualifier name. This would be a complete 'no no' in continuous text but on signs it can work if done carefully. In the upper example the qualifier is mathematically centred; in the lower one it is visually centred in the appropriate space.

92 Greenford
IRON BRIDGE

92 Iron Bridge
UXBRIDGE ROAD

Where it does and doesn't work. In the upper example the primary name has no descender and so the typesize has been enlarged. In the lower example the primary name does have a descender and so it is at the standard 70mm cap height.

308 Lea Interchange Temple Mills Lane

308 Lea Interchange
TEMPLE MILLS LANE

This destination would have caused a lot of problems in the old style layout, a theoretical example of which is illustrated above.

The electronic era starts

The 'Smart Blind' display boxes provided for many years by McKenna's have some sophisticated electronic features, and so it is a moot point to say they did not start the electronic era. However, as far as the actual displays themselves are concerned, they belong in an earlier one, still using printed roller blinds — and in my opinion still without equal for definition.

For years there has been a will within the bus industry to move to dot-matrix displays in London, as used in almost all of the rest of the country. The advantages are seen to be greater flexibility when buses move garage and reduced costs in eliminating continual updates, requiring printing of replacement blinds and physical visits to garages to repace the contents of the Smart Blind boxes. Dot matrix displays have been around for a long time and have become very reliable too — so why the delay?

The short answer is that the size of the dots and the distance separating them (known as 'pitch') has not provided high enough resolution standards and in turn legibility. Transport for London has a justifiably high reputation for quality in this respect and in simple terms, the quality of dot matrix has just not been good enough. During the two years creating the library, and with continual updates when new destinations were being required, I continued to monitor developments.

The e-paper trials

Readers are probably familiar with hand-held book readers such as 'Kindle'. These use a technology that requires no power at all while displaying a static image; it is only required to change the image, and as such these devices consume meagre battery power.

In 2015 TfL decided to test this product against printed roller blinds, though there were challenges to overcome. Apart from the attraction of low power consumption on the bus, the definition (resolution) was so close to a printed blind that no sane person would want to try and tell the difference. If this sounded 'too good to be true' then it was sensible to find out.

Two Smart Blind boxes were needed on the bus front, one for the destination and one for the route number. As I have noted earlier, these are too narrow and have caused all manner of compromises for the legibility of the contents.

At that time e-paper screens were only available in a limited range of sizes, and none big enough for a front display on a bus. The black 'letterbox' masking on the front glass of the bus is there to hide the frames of the blind boxes and this would be the first hurdle for the e-paper screens. Using the largest screens, three were needed, landscape, side-by-side. This was slightly wider than the destination and route number boxes together. Furthermore, the e-paper screens each had a frame and placing them side-by-side caused an unusable gap of 14mm, making legible displays even more difficult as the gaps had to be avoided and built into the layout. The human trait of assuming all was well before, and therefore copying it without considering new circumstances, became manifest. By the time I produced the required displays, the screens had been fitted and lamentably the route number screen was still separated from the two for the destination for no good reason.

'Marble Arch' has been compromised by having to avoid the join. Condensed lettering had to be used where Medium was fine on a printed blind. The compromise also caused an unsightly gap between the destination and route number.

In this example fitting a word space around the join between two 32-inch screens was unavoidable.

These examples demonstrate that designing legible layouts and manufacturing the display products are two separate processes requiring two separate skill sets.

Two portrait 13½-inch screens were needed for the rear route number and avoiding the join caused many problems. Above are the two displays as produced and below how the software people decided they would mangle them.

All destinations and route numbers would be required for all routes the chosen double-deck buses could operate on. The intention had been to equip two at Cricklewood garage.

My layouts were produced in London and then sent over the internet to the hardware and software company which was based in Slovenia.

With one bus equipped I visited the garage to check all was well — which sadly it wasn't. This was not surprising as it was the first attempt at something quite new.

Out in the courtyard, by the magic of electronics and a hand-held device, the layouts were received from Slovenia and controlled remotely to the bus.

Naturally there was also a selection pad inside the cab for the driver.

The outcome

The displays all worked within the constraints that the hardware permitted, though it became obvious that there was plenty of potential for operator error, mainly caused by the destinations having to be in two pieces. A more fundamental problem existed though.

Kindles are of course going to be read from close quarters, just like the books they seek to emulate. Though this is not the way I would want to read a book, because of several limitations I cannot go into here, great attention has clearly been given to the typography in this context. The background is very light grey and the text very dark grey — but not black. If these hand-held devices had truly black text on a truly white background, and even with the matte finish of the surface to reduce glare, the extreme contrast would make reader fatigue occur very quickly.

Aside from the joins in the screens, which thankfully TfL adjudged unacceptable, the contrast between the black background and white lettering was poor. The manufacturers in all fairness cranked this up as much as the product would allow, but it still fell short of printed blinds, exacerbated by the reflective front glass of the bus, which remains a major problem with modern bus design.

The trials did not last that long and as far as I know only one bus got equipped. As I understand it, the problem with the joins and lack of contrast were not the proverbial nail in the coffin. When TfL asked how robust the hardware was, and how it would stand up to being bumped about for up to twenty hours a day, no satisfactory answer was forthcoming. This is one of the major drawbacks of being a pioneer. These screens had been designed for a quite different purpose and were being asked to perform a radically different task.

The bus reverted to printed roller blinds.

As the destination was two screens, it was of course possible for each to display anything it was fed. The black and white images on these screens were also reversible. I must emphasise that at no time did I see this sort of thing when the bus was in service.

Dot-Matrix LED displays

Hanover Displays has been a market leader in this technology for many years and supply bus operators throughout the country and overseas, though had not penetrated London for reasons noted earlier.

The benefits of LED (Light Emitting Diode) dot-matrix displays include their relative simplicity to manufacture and operate and of course that they do not suffer from the lengthy process of updating and manual labour at the garages that is seen as the big drawback of printed roller blinds. Potentially huge quantities of destinations are available at the 'flick of a switch' on any bus thus equipped. Is this another 'too good to be true' story? Well, yes and no — depending on how you weigh up ease of use by the provider, against ease of reading by the recipient.

I said earlier that the legibility mantra is: 'spacing, spacing, spacing' and that still applies with dot-matrix. However, a major additional factor of legibility with this technology is resolution. To put it in simple terms, what size are the dots and how far apart are they? For the benefit of readers unfamiliar with this, dot-matrix is a simple grid pattern of LEDs on a board and the letters displayed are formed by switching on the appropriate LEDs (dots) and leaving the remaining ones unilluminated. The apparent resulting characters will be quite crude in shape where the dots are big and the spacing (pitch) is wide.

Outside London dot-matrix bus displays are ubiquitous, and some are, not to put too fine a point on it, terrible. This is caused by two factors: firstly, the larger the dots and the greater the pitch, the worse the legibility; secondly, the less the operator understands the plight of the reader the more widespread these displays have become.

The obvious benefit of larger and therefore fewer dots, is that they are cheaper. I'll leave it at that.

TfL takes the plunge

Having visited Hanover's factory in Lewes I explained why they had so far failed to attract TfL and was gratified to see that other LED boards were available, with much smaller dots and closer pitch. These of course came at a price. It matters not a jot what is printed on a roller blind, the cost will be the same, but more dots means more money. The price escalates notably for higher resolution, and the result still does not compare well with printed blinds. Furthermore, the closer these are seen, as on a side blind by the entrance, the harder they are to read.

In order to show TfL a viable product, the lettering had to be as defined as possible and using my four Johnston bus blind variants. Hanover had experimented with New Johnston, which is quite unsuited to bus blinds, because it is too heavy and there are no condensed variants at all — it is actually not possible to make most destinations DDA compliant.

There were technical challenges to get my layouts onto Hanover's boards but we found a way between us.

Having shown Leon Daniels and Tom Cunnington of TfL the best resolutions possible a meeting was set up in February 2018 to arrange a trial. Six new buses at West Ham garage would be equipped with the co-operation of Stagecoach — front and rear boards with 3mm pitch and the side entrance board with 2mm.

I was keen to take advantage of a one-piece front display board, especially as there was about 150mm of dead width between the two Smart Blind boxes that could now be used. Unfortunately this did not materialise and all I got was the same width of the two boxes overall, without the gap. A real opportunity lost.

Designing the layouts

The single piece board provided new challenges. Even with 3mm pitch (outside London they are commonly noticeably greater and so far more crude) using my Johnston Ultra Condensed would not be easy to read; this was also true for the 2mm pitch side board that required qualifiers, in anything other than Medium.

I have illustrated the restricted width of Smart Blind route number boxes earlier. With a single front board it would be possible to optimize the choice from the four Johnston variants when combining destination and route number. This is not the magic elixir. From the four typefaces and two lettering sizes, there are actually 32 possible combinations for destination and route number; adding the exclusion of some variants with long names not being feasible in Ultra Condensed, great care was needed.

East Ham   **474**

Beckton Station   **474**

London City Airport   **473**

Wanstead Park Stn.   **330**

A few examples of front displays showing the importance of keeping a visual balance between the destination and the route number. The abbreviation was introduced to avoid using Ultra Condensed. I only abbreviate when absolutely necessary and when the abbreviation is widely known.

At the time of writing, December 2020, many more buses have been equipped with these displays, though the circumstances of the Covid19 pandemic have caused things to go off track. TfL intends to resolve this in due course. For now, there are some very unsatisfactory displays on the road outside my control.

TFT/LCD displays

Thin-Film Transistor is a type of LCD (Liquid Crystal Display) screen, a technology similar to that used for many computer monitors and televisions.

TfL approached Navaho Technologies of Brocken-hurst to test their product on a single-decker. Such screens have been used inside buses for many years but until then none outside.

The main advantage of these screens is their high resolution which, in context, is every bit as good as a printed blind. They have ambient light control which adjusts the brightness according to the prevailing conditions, though McKenna's Smart Blind boxes have this feature too, as do Hanover's dot-matrix boards. Their disadvantage, I am informed, is rather high power consumption and, as with e-paper, unknown longevity and robustness.

Having been introduced to the company at the launch of TfL's TA1 tri-axle bus for route 12 in November 2018 (equipped with Hanover's dot-matrix boards), I was invited to visit Navaho's factory at TfL's request. Navaho had produced the destination and route number displays themselves and had the same problem as McKenna's, in that the route number wouldn't fit and had to be distorted. Fortunately the destinations on the route operated were short enough to not cause a problem.

Subsequent to visiting Waterloo garage, I supplied them with the correct layouts and, as far as I know, the bus is still in service.

Of the various technologies available, subject to rigorous testing, it is my view that these screens are the only challenge to printed, if the passengers' needs are regarded as paramount.

Once again, what was done in the past with the restrictions of the time, has been replicated unnecessarily: two separate boxes. This photograph was taken at the Coach & Bus exhibition at the NEC in October 2018.

13 STOPS FOR LONDON BUSES
Ivan Bennett

From the 1950s all vitreous enamel bus stop flags, route display boats and route plates were principally manufactured by Burnham Signs, a sign manufacturer in Lower Sydenham, although Garnier & Company of Hackney were also a significant supplier of vitreous enamel signage across London Transport (both were later acquired and equipment transferred to Stocksigns in Redhill by 2004). Garnier generally manufactured flat plate components including the pre-war framed GENERAL flag. Burnham's held all the original press tooling for the 'self cleaning' model designed by publicity officer Christian Barman's team from 1948 which replaced the earlier double-sided flat vitreous enamel and brass framed model, the frame over time trapping dust.

The bus stop sign remains a pressed, folded and welded low carbon steel fabrication finished to prescribed TfL and British Standards for Vitreous Enamel. The unit is finished using a thin layer of opaque frit (water-based clay slurry) sprayed and silk screened in individual layers and fused at high temperature to the steel substrate providing a smooth glass-like finish. VE provides a high quality, colour fast long life graphical solution which is robust, scratch, UV, chemical and fire resistant, whilst being easy to clean and redress. Trueform continue to manage and fabricate all the steel work, whilst the specialist finishing is undertaken by A J Wells in Newport on the Isle of Wight.

In the late 1980s the Advertising & Publicity Department of London Regional Transport (henceforth referred to simply as London Transport or LT) had been experimenting with a simple low cost, lightweight bus stop design. It utilised semi-ridged printed boards retained within an aluminium 'flag' style frame mounted on a square section cream or grey coloured finished mild steel post with integral framework for accommodating timetable frames. Whilst it addressed the need for more flexible signing system, simple to maintain and different from anything that had been provided before, it lacked any particular identity, solidity or permanence. They quickly became 'grubby', using materials typically utilised by retailers and they were easily damaged. So in 1990 Advertising & Publicity asked JEDCo product design consultants to consider potential options to 'modulise' the display of route numbers, due to the increasing number of service changes. This resulted in a series of initial sketch ideas and scale model of a modular 'boat' system to hang beneath existing flags.

An early LGOC prototype hand painted timber flag fixed to a gas light street column in a photo dated 1920.

A late 1980s LT Advertising & Publicity designed bus stop flag and route display printed on a range of different size flat Foamex panels retained within an aluminium square profile painted frame with separate printed self adhesive route labels known as E-Stickers. Bus stop codes were untidily applied to flag faces until dedicated plates were introduced in the 1990s.

Simultaneously Pentagram architectural and design consultancy, had been re-engaged by London Transport Advertising to review their recently introduced street furniture range. Pentagram had previously been employed by LTAdshel in 1982 to design a new range of shelters which went on to form the 'Townplan 2000 System' of street furniture. This was built around the Sigma shelter with its generous full curved overhanging dome roof and visually 'soft' extruded framework and perch seat, it also included a bench, litter bin, fingerpost and freestanding advertising displays, which receive commendation from the Design Council in 1984. However, the Townplan suite of furniture should have included a free-standing bus stop, but by 1990 it had still not been progressed.

Information management should be at the centre of the provision of bus stops, but whilst publicity had been managed by London Transport's Publicity Office it had been supported by a Works & Building Department at Parsons Green until its closure in 1986, when the responsibility for infrastructure had been passed down to the Bus Operating Districts and privatised operators. So by 1991 London Transport, anticipating the confusion of the privatisation and even potential deregulation of the bus network, set up the Bus Passenger Infrastructure (BPI) Department to manage the city's bus infrastructure to ensure there remained a unified provision of bus stops, shelters, stations and stands. To catalogue its roadside assets BPI established a computerised database known as CALMS (Computer Assisted Location & Management of Stops) to manage both physical components and the dissemination of passenger information such as timetables, route maps and service schedules to various delivery partners within London Buses.

A year later Fitch, a design consultancy company, was engaged by London Buses Group Marketing to develop a comprehensive information strategy covering corporate branding, marketing, liveries, publicity and signage. During this period JEDCo had been employed by Dick Cordey, General Manager of BPI, to provide a design resource, relieving the "burden of day to day design problems", maintaining a regular dialogue and contributing to providing a cost-effective and coherent design strategy ideally aiming to achieve an evolutionary programme towards the "ideal bus stop of the future". This included compiling a catalogue of as-built drawings for all existing components utilised across the reunited network of 16,000 stops, whilst reviewing maintenance methods. Nearly 100 drawings were completed illustrating the myriad of historical and now inconsistent and uneconomical combination of low quality parts re-enforcing the business case for the development of the 'ideal' bus stop, establishing physical performance requirements and constraints.

Full size model of Pentagram proposed bus stop design illustrating the semicircular flag with stop name and cantilevered single sided double 36in publicity display case. This display option was not compliant with the DfT Traffic Signs Manual design standards projecting over the pavement potentially causing a hazard for children, wheelchair and pushchair users and for the blind and partially sighted. The display was considered to be too large, obstructive and prone to graffiti and fly-posting with its blank road facing aspect, whilst its flat top wouldn't have deterred rubbish and water.

JEDCo had already completed another piece of work earlier in the year for London Transport's Passenger Information at Bus Stops (PIBS) Planning Manager Stephen Balogh. This PIBS review focused around the design and ergonomic specification for the proposed LED matrix display and street furniture application of the Real Time Information system branded as 'Countdown'. Recommendations included establishing an optimum size of a display, minimum character height and layout, positioning and nominal viewing distances. In turn the outline design for its accommodation within passenger shelters and possibility of integrating it within a freestanding bus stop. This resulted in the now generic MKI display case, with its bayonet fixing and freestanding bus stop unit (FSU), and the first fifty installations along route 18, including nine FSUs.

JEDCo arranged for a factory visit to Trueform Engineering to review progress in the design and development of the Countdown FSU with Balogh and Cordey, where Keith Clark, Trueform's original General Manager, showed the team around their then modest facilities to discuss progress with the supply of the units. Cordey, who was a stickler for value, kept being distracted by other pieces he recognised as passenger shelter parts. BPI had been purchasing components for non-advertising passenger shelters through their LT/Adshel Partnership and he asked whether Trueform would be interested in supplying directly at a more economical price. There is no doubt that those early relationships informed the future growth and development of Trueform, and influenced BPI to separate the supply, installation and maintenance of their growing shelter estate. Ultimately this improved supply and created a new culture and sense of 'ownership' by the supplier and responsibility for its delivery and subsequent supply, installation and maintenance over the next three decades.

This activity enabled BPI to issue its bus stop design brief which emphasised that any new design must maximise the benefits of work done by London Transport's post-war designers. It called for a system that would enhance the business's perceived image, information provision, improve the manageability of replacing information, uphold standards of safety for passengers, pedestrians, road users and staff, allow expedient cost effective maintenance, reducing inconvenience in the loss of services, whilst asking the designer "to take the bus stop into the future".

Preliminary sketches for the design and development of free-standing passenger information displays beyond the shelter mounted option inevitably involved consideration of future bus stop furniture possibilities. Considerations included reducing obstruction for pedestrians whilst maintaining passenger and driver sight lines. Drawn by JEDCo Product Designers in February 1992.

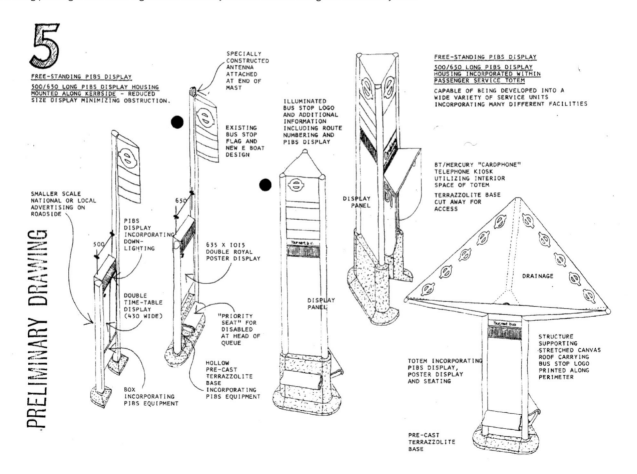

The bus stop hadn't been reviewed for forty years, albeit some branding work by Misha Black's Design Research Unit in 1972. Elements of the original sign system were in need of replacement immediately, whilst manufacturing methods had changed and new materials and processes had become available.

However, whilst Jeremy Rewse-Davies, London Transport's Design Director, had commissioned a separate study by Pentagram to design a bus stop system from scratch, BPI as asset owner had retained JEDCo to complete their project as an evolutionary, rather than a wholly new venture. JEDCo's proposal was based on value analysis of the existing collection of pieces enabling the business to phase in any new components and refine ideas over a more economically pragmatic period. In May 1993 a meeting with the Bus Stop Design & Development Steering Group chaired by London Transport' s Director of Trading selected JEDCo's proposal.

JEDCo and Fitch began to work in close collaboration throughout the summer to make the sign system a reality, managing a huge amount of detail to establish the physical manifestation and progressive disclosure of information on the street. JEDCo immersed itself in site visits, shadowing contractors and BPI roadside staff, visiting suppliers and assessing numerous proprietary sign systems. By November the steering group approved the design development drawings, although there were last minute changes from BPI when they saw photographs of scale models in advance of the presentation. JEDCo had finished them in the previously specified Bronze Green, which had been implemented during the LT/Adshel Insignia passenger shelters programme, rather than a more contemporary use of natural satin anodised aluminium which was felt to be neutral and an unchallengeable colour finish which would age well.

Following the value analysis of existing equipment several elements of the original designs began to inform the appearance of the bus stop. This included the existing style of 'self cleaning' vitreous enamel flag, which was seen with its high quality finish to offer a more contemporary feel, whilst reinforcing the connection in the use of its vitreous enamel material as an intrinsic contribution to the design language which had become synonymous with London as reassuring, bright and familiar. In addition it was decided to retain the recently designed publicity timetable display frame. The original LRT frame – made up of mahogany, with brass reinforced corners, zinc backing, glass glazing and brass pegs for mounted punched paper publicity was expensive and prone to damage.

The original bus stops did nothing to distinguish one site from another; if you got off at the wrong stop you may have no real idea of where you were or what general direction the buses serving the stop were

going. Site-specific naming would solve this passenger dilemma, and displaying stop names opened up some significant features to come. The Fitch-designed Bus Stop Sign System, published in 1994, for the first time addressed the users' principal concerns, 'where am I' or 'where is the bus going?'

A single service change may require the reordering of every number on the flag, since the routes appear in numerical and alphanumerical order. JEDCo devised a contemporary take on the framed plates, in the form of a automotive grade polycarbonate self pigmented moulding with a projecting button on its reverse. This button slides into a corresponding keyhole slot, equally spaced on the new steel fabricated boats. The boats were in turn available in three modular configurations and can be stacked to provide space to display up to eighteen services. Whilst route number tiles were more expensive than vinyl they provided greater longevity, were tamper resistant in sitting flush under the flag, and could be infinitely and quickly re-arranged, seasonally and even temporarily removed and stored offering considerable savings. They were also recyclable, unlike vinyl.

Preliminary sketches for the design and development of future bus stop furniture with considerations for more contemporary totem style installations around a triangular profile, with options for different sizes of signage, display and street lighting column mounting. Drawn by JEDCo Product Designers, September 1993.

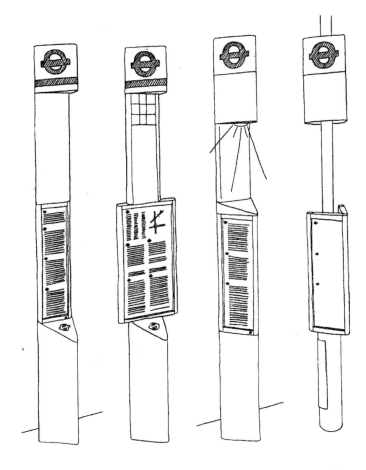

Part of a range of scale models of the proposed bus stop design showing a free-standing 'Countdown' unit and smaller HD digital colour 'Countdown' bus stop variation presented in 1994. The latter variation was not prototyped and built until 2003.

Although they are more expensive than self adhesive vinyl (SAV) E-Stickers they soon paid for themselves in the reduced replacement cost of SAV, whilst ensuring a neater more legible and consistent numerical/alpha-numerical display is maintained. The E-Stickers had been produced for individual stops until 1999, when the TfL Network was finally upgraded to accept the new tile system. Initial batches had been introduced in spring 1994.

The original set of cast concrete post mould tools, had fallen into unsatisfactory states of repair and suffered from poor design alterations making for a series of inconsistent details requiring on-site amendments. JEDCo went on to employ Colebrand Ltd, specialist concrete structural consultants, to review the condition of the tooling, their handling, installation method and to propose a new performance specification.

The new material was extruded aluminium with a 'natural' satin anodised finish, making it more resilient and considerably easier to clean than concrete. The posts were now extremely lightweight and completely interchangeable. However, the principal reason for adopting extruded aluminium was the possibility to run utilities wiring through the post. The 3.5 metre high extruded aluminium post was light in weight, safer in the event of impact and easy to clean.

For some locations the design begins sub-surface with its 450mm deep socket foundation into which the post and its reinforcing spigot is plugged. An alternative shallow foundation plate is available where there are underground obstructions replacing the structurally dubious steel fabricated 'Cradle' previously used to support the cast concrete posts. There were significant concerns about the reliability of this method, particularly as posts were frequently knocked down following repeated wing mirror strikes and concrete fatigue. The new socket provided opportunities to include ducted electrical and telecom utilities to be run into the stop, allowing timetables to be illuminated and possible later adaptation for electronic display systems such as Countdown. Ideas were also presented for at-stop features and amenities: ticketing (rather like a retail receipt printer), smart card validator supporting the Harrow Smart Photocard project and a smaller

Part of the range of scale models of the proposed bus stop design showing a possible variation. Known as the 'statement stop', it retained the inviting curved style and many of the existing bus stop parts. It was proposed to support services within busier town centres, interchanges and regional bus hubs enhancing the visual presence of the bus stop in often visually congested landscapes. This design enabled twenty-one routes to be displayed with options for integrated 'Countdown' display or clock (not shown), whilst the flag could have been internally illuminated with proposals to manufacture it from a printed translucent polycarbonate pressure forming. Whilst none were built, the signage and publicity display components were utilised for surface mounted wall applications.

display within the publicity frame inspired by retail shopping tills. Further sketches included ideas for courtesy lighting, improving overall recognition, safety and legibility, illuminated flag displays, flashing beacon for hailing a bus, public address system converting the newly available Countdown information text to speech and options for the recently introduced REACT key fob audio trigger system developed by the RNIB. Integral priority perch seating, help point button and street furniture options provided segregated waiting points using marked bollards to manage queuing.

Safety was a key feature and the lightweight structure was designed to progressively bend and absorb impact with reduced risk to passers-by. Today, one post is typically lost every day due to vehicle impact, but now 90 per cent of vehicular impacts result in the simple replacement of the deformed post rather than the wholesale placement of the pole, flag and information cases. The range included standard 3.5 metre height and reduced 2.1 metre post for non-flagged Hail & Ride units deployed at either end of a Hail & Ride section of a route. These shorter posts also formed one half of

the future free-standing 'Countdown' unit FSU upgrade kit designed in 1997, although funding for further installations had now dwindled with most units being fitted prudently to shelters to reduce costs.

The post was originally finished at ground level with a two part cast exposed and pigmented grey basalt aggregate concrete moulded base. Its colour and texture were considered to be more resilient against build-up of grime, abrasion from street cleaning machines and urine. Whilst for some it was simply a decorative flourish, the base offered a high degree of colour contrast against the predominantly lighter finished pavement surface. It provided a tactile marker for blind and partially sighted cane users and also deflected baby buggies and wheelchairs – and even children previously prone to bumping into the projecting timetables above. The base was also designed to cover the more unsightly and clumsy reinstatement around its foundations, whilst covering its sub-surface fixings and optional cable entry. The base is now manufactured using a more resilient pigmented composite of recycled rubber and PVC compression moulding.

Trueform Engineering, based in Hayes, was a family owned steel fabrication company already supplying passenger shelter components as a subcontractor to Queensbury (a previous supplier to More O'Ferrell Adshel) which had already been working with JEDCo on various other London Transport signage and display projects. JEDCo chose to continue to work with them for the initial pre-production prototyping of the bus stop, primarily due to their location within convenient reach of their studio in Weybridge and on the M25 orbital and M4 corridors serving London.

After a great deal of effort the initial Design & Development Stage of the project was completed on the last day of the financial year, the first aluminium bus stop being erected early evening of 31 March 1994 outside Richmond station. Trueform complete the installation in miserable weather and under the inquisitive scrutiny of commuters and staff involved in the project, with the foundations having been completed earlier by the Colebrand specialist concrete team. This was quickly followed by others throughout Richmond and Ilford town centres and along King Henry's Drive into New Addington. This proved a challenging environment and enabled the design team to address weaknesses in the components' assembly, with installations having been shot, burned, stolen and even tied to the rear of a bus whilst on stand, subsequently removing its bonnet, leaving a rather bemused driver.

Subsequent special installations were undertaken for the City of London Corporation outside Guildhall on Gresham Street (amusingly with notices stating that: 'This is not a Bus stop and is for exhibition only'), and a special black finished post at Piccadilly Circus for Westminster City Council (WCC) for consultation purposes. The black finished version was requested as WCC had recently reviewed and published its Streetscape Design Guidelines and was keen for all (except Post Office, pillar boxes and original Phone kiosks) street furniture to be finished in black. The stop looked heavy and visually indistinguishable in the streetscape, whilst providing poor visual contrast particularly at night.

Keen to avoid a time-consuming London-wide consultation the Design Working Group formally invited the Royal Fine Arts Commission (RFAC), who had shown interest and recognised the important of the impact of the bus stop on London's streetscape, to a presentation. After an introduction by Rewse-Davies, JEDCo made a presentation at 55 Broadway with various sketches and scale models. The RFAC subsequently congratulated the group for their comprehensive design approach, awarding it commendation, with the only contentious detail being the finish of the base. However, the team had prepared a few alternative samples of texture and colour enabling JEDCo to persuade everyone to accept the preferred option.

Following competitive tender, in 1996 Trueform Engineering began its first contract to supply, build and maintain bus stops for Bus Infrastructure, and whilst printing was initially subcontracted the company soon appreciated that due to the bespoke nature of the bus stop (and later shelters) they looked to bring as many services in-house as possible. A total of 3000 bus stops had already been equipped with the Fitch style named flags and boats beneath, and to complete the network expediently Trueform invested in printing facilities to provide a Just-In-Time delivery process, reducing possible duplication and delivery times, whilst addressing inevitable mistakes and late amendments. However, it wasn't all without its challenges and 'teething problems' were encountered with inconsistent tolerances, incorrect combination of fixings and poor handling by installation contractors. Fingerprints, scratched paintwork, peeling vinyl and splashed concrete do not imply a sense of quality and care.

Successful product design stems from a fusion of three criteria: aesthetics, appropriateness and economics, but design should ideally reflect a personality, and a commitment to high quality which has made elements of London's transport design synonymous with London itself. Frank Pick said of bus stops that they should not be mere poles, but "the modest representation of an organisation offering comfort and visual pleasure." The common emphasis in design is all too often concerned only with its durability and functionality, which can be rather austere. Alan Murray, Head of Premises Development, Bus Passenger Infrastructure said "Whilst the casual user may have scarcely noticed any difference, the client now has a distinctive fresh and effective advertisement for services, which should be more durable, simpler to maintain, safer, and easier to instal than the original, all within acceptable costs."

The new bus stop was exhibited by RIBA and the LT Museum in 1995 for the exhibition 'Designed for London, 150 Years of Transport Design', whilst The Design Museum Review Gallery 1996-97 and Stanley Picker Gallery at Kingston University 2006 have also recognised the contribution the bus stop has made towards design and iconography of London. The subsequent solar power enhancements went on to win commendations from The Bus Industry Awards and the Institute of Lighting Engineers in 2004.

A consequence of the back-lighting is the need to have single sided printed media, and as a result this helped reinforce other developments to introduce Stop Specific Timetables. However, JEDCo recommended the use of more light transmissive media (to maximise light output) used extensively across retail. Sadly this has never been progressed, as publicity continues to be funded by TfL Marketing rather than Bus Infrastructure and, as such, illuminated media remains paper based and compromised. Despite the Bus Stop Information

Steering Group's initial rejection of possible solar or wind power generation following completion of the mains powered installations, a decision was made to design and develop a self contained and more sustainable powered solution, resulting in a new design brief being issued to JEDCo and other design consultants to respond to.

By the late 1990s Jonathan Morley at Trueform had established a design-led culture there, guiding the business to make further significant investment in new manufacturing capabilities.

JEDCo's design response included working with Trueform along with another customer, Sartech Engineering of Tadworth. JEDCo went on to design and test various potential roadside energy generation solutions, including wind turbines, subsurface pedestrian activated pressure sensitive piezoelectric and hydraulic dynamos, and even a customer activated wind-up model. All of these were to illuminate the timetable publicity display and flag sign using the latest lighting technologies, including the first generation of high-flux white LEDs, focused lenses, acrylic and multilayered film light guides, Electroluminescent (EL) panels, reflectors and reflective coatings. The first installations at Eaton Square and along the route 65 corridor serving Ealing to Kingston town centres offered a range of street environments and lighting conditions.

Experimental pre-dressed modular publicity panel being fitted improved the overall quality of presentation at the bus stop. The panel also reduced glazing damage, reinforcing the rear of the glass, although this idea went on to be replaced by an impact absorbing foam backed panel known as the Apology panel.

Modular route E-Tiles being fitted on the Boat using the key-hole slots. The Mobility services were subsequently re-coloured black text on a tangerine coloured tile to improve recognition and consistency with other London Transport mobility information.

Modular route display known as an E9 Boat being fitted to the underside of the Flag.

By 2008, 4500 posts had been upgraded to include solar photovoltaic (PV) modules mounted to the top of the post over the flag providing sufficient power to light the flag sign and rear illuminate the publicity display panels from 'dusk till dawn'. Solar technology can provide adequate energy to improve the visibility of the stop flag and inclusive access to publicity, whilst enhancing the bus stop environment, ensuring passengers feel 'safer' and more valued. Solar energy is safer than mains connection as there is no danger to the public, is cheaper to install and is environmentally responsible. Some considerable effort had been spent in reducing the visual impact of the previously accepted norm of solar panels being positioned 50 degrees facing south. It was felt that this engineered solution was 'ugly' with its clumsy brackets and unsightly and vulnerable exposed cabling. JEDCo's solution was to integrate the PV into a curved canopy structure spread over the flag, accommodating luminaires to illuminate the flag surface beneath, whilst cabling and connectors could be hidden inside, resulting in a more sympathetic design. Market research undertaken during the trial showed that illumination of the bus stops helped users feel safer. It also discovered that people liked the aesthetic with its canopy lighting and rear illuminated display, whilst being pleased to learn that solar power was being used. However, the programme was cancelled following a review by the GLA and the then new Mayoral administration later that year.

Meanwhile, Trueform had continued to invest in resources to cover their increasingly diverse transport sector customers, including branding, wayfinding, ticket vending, and even manufacturing pre-production cycle hire station furniture for TfL. JEDCo went on to design various other supplementary bus stop components including temporary 'dolly' bus stops, temporary closure hoods and timetable panels, high definition electronic timetable displays in 2004, and

Mother and child reading rear LED edge lit illuminated timetable publicity at a solar powered and LED illuminated bus stop, illustrating the improved legible access to information and identification of the bus stop in low urban lit conditions.
The second illustration shows the components making this up.

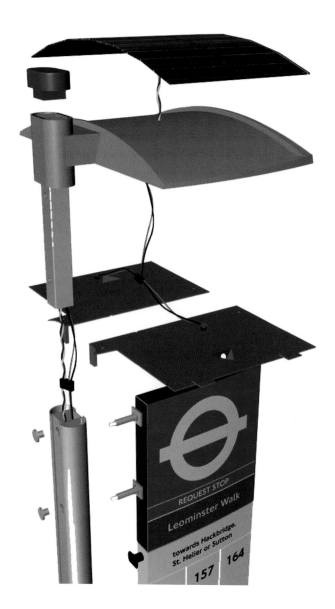

Above left: The latest design of flag, restoring the words BUS STOP to the bar.

Above: In 2014, for the Year of the Bus, the Lego style flag was posted outside Hamley's.

Below: Today, bus stop flags have embraced services not traditionally associated with them, including London black taxis.

even an internally illuminated bus stop flag providing greater recognition, improved presentation and with less power.

There were sadly-missed opportunities, principally not continuing development of the bus stop to include more relevant technology-driven communication media, such as digital displays utilising the business's own RTI system as previously identified in the earlier 1990s. Whilst ideas have been trialled and mocked up, this involved a lot of 'goodwill' from partners and contractors with little subsequent commitment from the business due to a lack of continued investment and specialist departments within TfL competing for survival, responsibility of assets and control of particular disciplines. Incremental change is more modest, even invisible, but new businesses and administrations like substantial, dynamic, even culturally disruptive changes and the bus had become sidelined as being prosaic.

Unlike a railway network, once the bus has passed by there is little evidence of the network. The bus stop provides that physical manifestation of the route nominally every 400 metres; like beacons they mark its course, drawing you along at a reassuringly regular pace. Unlike most county cities, the metropolitan cities of the world generally provide more consistently branded infrastructure and if you're a Londoner you're spoilt with such a distinctively recognisable brand. When you've been away from London you know when you're almost home: you reassuringly pass your first London Buses bus stop.

Above left: The latest design of flag, restoring the words BUS STOP to the bar.

Above: In 2014, for the Year of the Bus, the Lego style flag was posted outside Hamley's.

Below: Today, bus stop flags have embraced services not traditionally associated with them, including London black taxis.

MAKING LONDON BUSES ACCESSIBLE
Andrew Braddock

Though I had two spells of working for London Transport (later Transport for London), I was never directly employed in the Bus Department of LT or what became London Buses Limited. Hailing from north London, I apparently came close to being born on a trolleybus on route 607 near Hillingdon, when my mother was visiting a family friend during the late stages of her pregnancy - herein, perhaps, lay the origins of my fondness for the trolleybus as well as the tram – it, too, being a hugely practical means of moving large numbers of people about in cities, using clean electric traction.

The family moved to Somerset where I attended Wells Cathedral School and in 1964/65 I went to the Technical College in Bath at the start of what should have been a career in surveying. Not knowing what I wanted to do for work, and not wishing to go to University, I had taken the advice of a Great Uncle, who had once been Borough Surveyor of Wood Green, and duly joined the Western Region of British Rail at Paddington as a Junior Estate & Rating Surveyor Trainee. Less than a

year later I had transferred my allegiance to London Transport in a similar role but by the end of 1968 I had joined the Bristol Omnibus Company, to be nearer the young lady I later married and who has since put up with me for more than fifty years!

At Bristol Omnibus I ended up as District Traffic Superintendent (Swindon) in 1973 and from there I went in 1976 to London Country Bus Services as Area Manager (South) and three years later became Field Operations Manager for the entire "Polo mint" shaped company. From May 1984 I was Traffic Manager at Alder Valley and on the division of that company prior to privatisation I went with the northern part of its territory to create "The Bee Line", later becoming the new company's General Manager.

In my second period of working for LT from 1991, I was responsible as Head of the Unit for Disabled Passengers for ensuring that bus and rail services took account of the needs of mobility-impaired people, which was one of London Regional Transport's statutory duties from its inception in 1984. At Alder Valley I had

This Leyland National Mobility Bus operated by Capital Citybus was typical of the full-size vehicles deployed on these special services. This view is in Ilford High Road, June 1992.

Artist's impression of a Mercedes-Benz O405N low-floor bus adapted for the UK rule of the road.

been involved in operating some wheelchair-accessible Leyland Nationals which were a specialised adjunct to its private hire business, the company's central repair works having devised a lengthy portable ramp to get wheelchairs on board. Some of these vehicles – by now fitted with mechanical lifts at the front door - were subsequently used on "CareLine", the UK's first scheduled bus service with access for wheelchair-users but open to all, which The Bee Line ran between Heathrow Airport and central London with some Department of Transport funding.

I had also served on the National Bus Company's working group – chaired by the late Claudia Flanders – charged with meeting the needs of disabled people.

Claudia was the widow of Michael Flanders, of Flanders & Swann fame – creators of the splendid "big six-wheeler scarlet-painted London Transport diesel-engined 97-horsepower Omnibus" – who had been a wheelchair-user for most of his life.

As an American, Claudia was well aware that during the 1970s it became common in the United States for the then standard types of high-floor step-entrance city buses to be fitted with lifts so that wheelchair-users could board and alight, in response to growing pressure for disabled people to be given access to public transport. This led to federal legislation mandating wheelchair access to all bus and rail services.

During my first few weeks at 55 Broadway I met a

Artist's impression of the Wrights of Ballymena body design for low-floor buses prior to London placing an order for the first vehicles.

STEP

take a

don't

MAKING BUSES BETTER

because it's as easy as...

1 This bus actually kneels at stops, virtually eliminating the step at the entrance and exit doors, so you don't step up, you just step on.

2 There's no need to fold-up your child's buggy - just roll-on and off - even a double buggy or a shopping trolley.

3 Convenient and comfortable areas have been specially created for wheelchair-users and passengers with buggies and shopping.

Take a low floor bus

London's Buses Get on board

lot of aggrieved wheelchair-users who often chained themselves to Routemasters on the service 9 stand at Aldwych (much to the delight of the crews, who simply drank more tea while missing a round trip), and they clearly believed that their rights should take precedence over operational practicality, and the convenience of other passengers, by calling on LT to follow American practice.

Fortunately, there was some experience with enabling disabled Londoners to travel on regular timetabled services as the first "Mobility Bus" had taken to the streets in 1984. This also involved our old friend the Leyland National, this time with a platform lift at door two. Eligible disabled people could also use the pre-booked "Dial-a-Ride" minibus service, initially funded by the London Boroughs but an LT responsibility from 1986 (this too was operated with high-floor, lift-equipped vehicles), and they could have a "Taxicard" to make use of the growing number of wheelchair-accessible London black cabs. "Mobility Bus" represented an overlaid network of routes, operated in addition to conventional bus services – though at best each one ran on only two days a week with two journeys in each direction. As these services only catered for short local trips and both "Taxicard" and "Dial-a-Ride" were subject to trip limits, the real mobility of the users was restricted.

The experience with "Mobility Bus" (and "CareLine", which had become an LT responsibility with NBC privatisation) amply demonstrated that use of lifts to provide wheelchair access was a time-consuming process, and for the intensive bus system in London (and other major European cities) a time of four or more minutes to board one wheelchair-user (with a similar alighting time further along the route) would have been unacceptable in terms of delay to the services and to other passengers.

I had a particular interest in low-floor buses, developed in Germany in the late 1970s initially in the shape of airport transfer vehicles which were significantly wider than normal. The low-floor layout made entering and exiting with luggage much easier, and by 1977 Neoplan had built its first low-floor bus for use on scheduled urban services. The other major manufacturers (MAN, Mercedes-Benz and Setra) quickly followed suit. As a result of having no steps at the doorways these vehicles were quicker and safer for ambulant passengers to get on or off but did not, at that time, have any wheelchair access. In 1986, Munich became the first city to add a wheelchair ramp to its low-floor buses and this feature rapidly became widespread in Germany and in several other countries as the low-floor concept spread.

It was clear that low-floor buses, fitted with a powered ramp at door two and a rear-facing wheelchair space featuring an "ironing board" backrest as had become the German standard, would make it possible for a wheelchair-user to board or alight in less than one minute (with practice). This was to emerge as LT's preferred option to cope with the not unreasonable demands for people in wheelchairs to be given access to bus services.

It was also my strong belief that years of male-dominated public transport design had failed to even notice the struggle mothers with small children, folding baby-buggies and several bags of shopping had to get on (and off) our buses, and this traffic made up a considerably larger market than wheelchair-users!

The London Low-floor Bus Project was therefore set up in 1992 and the Department for Transport decided to sponsor a parallel introduction of low-floor buses on a route in North Tyneside. In London, the following five routes were selected involving five of the bus companies then owned by LT (and later privatised in 1994/95):-

101 (East London):	North Woolwich – Wanstead (Upton Park Garage)
120 (London United):	Hounslow – Northolt (Hounslow Garage)
144 (Leaside Buses):	Edmonton – Muswell Hill (Wood Green Garage)
186 (Metroline):	Brent Cross – Northwick Park (Harrow Weald Garage)
222 (CentreWest):	Hounslow – Uxbridge (Uxbridge Garage)

I was keen to ensure that the experience gained with significant numbers of low-floor buses in Germany should be passed on to my colleagues in the five London companies so we set up a series of study tours to Aachen, Düsseldorf, Essen, Hamburg and Kassel during 1993. Mixed groups of operating and engineering staff, including trade union representatives, participated and a very useful knowledge transfer took place. Through the contacts made, each of the five London operators was "twinned" with a German city in the Low-floor Bus Partnership or Niederflurbus Partnerschaft with a suitably-worded sticker fitted to all the low-floor buses of the partner fleets. The city of Dortmund was also involved, kindly agreeing that we could copy its "zip effect" vertical stripe with a broad arrow-head pointing to the low level of the bus floor.

Once the number of buses required was calculated, discussions began with potential manufacturers and for some time it looked as though a right-hand-drive adaptation of one or more continental vehicles would be selected, with Dutch Berkhof bodywork on an

Opposite: London Buses publicity setting out the advantages of the low-floor layout.

One of the Dennis Lance SLF/Wright Pathfinder 320 vehicles on the first route to go low-floor in January 1994.

MAN chassis (one such vehicle came to the UK as a demonstrator) and the Belgian Van Hool A300 integral as front-runners, but in time a combination of Wrights of Ballymena with both Dennis and Scania emerged with an acceptable package. A total of 68 vehicles was ordered from Dennis (38 Lance SLF chassis) and Scania (30 CRL113 chassis), all with the Northern Irish business's new "Pathfinder 320" bodywork (320 being the floor height of the front half of the bus in millimetres above road level). When built in late 1993 they were about 25% more expensive than the same size of conventional single-deck bus, but within three years the price premium had fallen to around 5% and soon afterwards to zero (in fact it eventually became more expensive to buy a step-entrance bus!).

In many ways these 68 vehicles were more like typical continental buses than previous single-deckers built for service in London. They were fitted, for example, with swing-plug doors and a German-made Bode powered ramp at door two and had London's first power-driven roller-blind destination displays.

The initial route (120) was converted in January 1994 and the other four followed during the year. The success of these buses resulted in the concept being extended and by 1996 Dennis had designed a low-floor version of the popular "Dart" midibus and barely a year later DAF, Dennis, Optare, Scania and Volvo were all producing low-floor double-deckers.

Though the introduction of low-floor buses was geared to meeting the needs of disabled people they dramatically improved the public transport offer for millions of non-disabled passengers – especially, as already mentioned, those travelling with small children, heavy baggage or shopping. Older passengers particularly benefited from the step-free doorways and "kneeling" suspension. Passenger numbers in London and elsewhere increased with the change to low-floor buses so these accessible vehicles made good business sense too! Furthermore, boarding and alighting accidents reduced due to the absence of steps in the doorways.

Soon after, throughout the UK, the bus industry was well on the way to achieving the goal of a fully-accessible bus system, which the Public Service Vehicles Accessibility Regulations 2000 required to be in place by 1 January 2016 (2017 for double-deck buses; 2020 for coaches), and the London fleet has been fully compliant since the end of 2005.

I was always proud of the way in which the vast majority of the drivers on the five initial low-floor routes quickly became accustomed to having wheelchair users travel on their bus, and in my frequent journeying around the capital it is now commonplace to see what we pioneered twenty-five years ago being an accepted fact. What makes it work so well is the simple access to and from the wheelchair space at door two and, from a difficult start, the reliability of the ramps that bridge the gap to the kerb at stops.

London Buses (LBL)

Low-down on new buses

During 1993/94, purpose-built low-floor buses were introduced in the Hounslow area on Routes 120 and 222, the first two of five planned routes.

The buses have special facilities for passengers with mobility problems, including a centre door which is accessible to wheelchair users and a single floor level inside the front half of the bus. The buses are also a benefit to other passengers, particularly those carrying shopping or with a small child in a pushchair. The struggle of folding up the pushchair while holding onto a toddler and the shopping is a thing of the past on a low-floor bus.

Inside the low-floor bus there is a wide gangway and plenty of brightly-coloured handrails to help passengers get to their seats easily. Some of the seats tip up to make extra room for heavy luggage.

There is space designed to accommodate one wheelchair between the centre and front doors. At the side of this space is a special bell push for wheelchair users to push before the bus reaches their stop. The driver then operates the ramp enabling the wheelchair user to get off the bus easily.

Passenger Lauren Lee finds the new buses make life much easier.

New-style bus stops give more information.

Stopping confusion

New bus stops are being tested in the Richmond and New Addington areas. Recent research showed that many people, particularly tourists, are deterred from using buses because they don't know which one to catch or how long they may have to wait for the next bus.

The new stops are designed to overcome those problems. They are named and clearly show in which direction the bus is travelling. Information on routes and bus times has been reorganised so that it is easy to read and understand.

Financial performance

London Buses' operating ratio improved by 5 per cent, largely as a result of preparing for privatisation. Operating costs per mile reduced to £2.41, on a price adjusted basis, excluding depreciation and renewals. This was mainly because of productivity measures introduced in late 1992 being reflected in the 1993/94 results. Mileage operated reduced as a result of tendering gains by independent operators and industrial action in April and May 1993.

From the introduction of the first horse-drawn buses in 1826, through the opening of the initial section of the Underground in 1863 and the inauguration of the city's electric tramway network in 1901, and right up to the 1980s little or no thought was given to the needs of passengers with reduced mobility. Yet among London's population of around eight million there are more than one million older people and a similar number with a disability that made it difficult or impossible to use public transport. Low-floor buses have made a huge difference to those two million and I firmly believe that a public transport system which is accessible to all is a mark of a civilised society.

Having explained my involvement in the low-floor revolution, I must confess to being a sizeable influence in the introduction of articulated buses in London, but before getting into the detail of that one-act tragedy I should explain my long-held views on the inadequacy of the uniquely British approach to bus design. Outside London a largely single-door layout leads to slow boarding and stage fare tickets bought with cash – often requiring change – certainly don't help. Worst of all is the packing of seats into every available space so that the only place to stand (which will always be necessary at the busiest times of the day) is the gangway, where you are bound to be in someone's way and your bottom is not far from an adjacent seated passenger's nose! Self-evidently, the low-floor pioneers and all their successors have a wheelchair space which can be used by standees when not required for its intended purpose. With more and more of the passenger market unable to climb the stairs, in my view the adherence to double-deck buses was unrealistic and it is interesting to see the extent to which – even at the height of the rush hours – they are running with empty seats upstairs but absolutely packed with standees on the lower deck.

Probably my most enduring exposure to the differences between the UK and continental Europe came as an 11-year old school exchange student when I went to stay with a family in Groningen in The Netherlands in the summer of 1960 and repeated the experience a year later at Leer in the far north of Germany. My hosts took me, respectively, to Amsterdam and Bremen for a weekend – in both cases by train, despite the fact that a family car was available. Even at the start of the 1960s, this struck me as different. The ease with which we travelled – fairly extensively – around the two cities was clearly different, too. I was very taken with the trams which, though looking pretty ancient for the most part, with just a smattering of streamlined articulated cars making their first appearance in each case, seemed to me then, and still more so now, to be an eminently sensible means of transport. Smooth-riding and extremely well-used, they were clearly creating their own priority long before the advent of the extensive reserved track layouts and new light rail extensions that have since typified both networks.

I could immediately sense a big difference between those two mainland European and typical UK cities. First, no double-decker buses! Second, streets which appeared predominantly to have been provided for trams and buses compared to streets filled with general traffic, and especially cars. And no traffic jams! The British approach to traffic management and public transport provision had suffered grievously from more than 50 years of following the American model of car dependence.

Continental operators were obsessed by the 1960s with the need to tailor public transport to the market it served. Their aim was to make it competitive with the car rather than to simply manage the decline greater car ownership implied as we did over here. To have introduced, as did London, a system in which the drivers also acted as conductors, selling tickets and giving change, that added about 25% to journey times and removed the consistency of them would have been unthinkable. That is why, when most mainland European operators took away the conductors, their job was given to the passengers. Time- rather than distance-based fares, usually one flat fare for a whole city, with unlimited transfer between vehicles; no on-board ticketing (unless it was from a self-serve machine or involved a much higher price for only the single-ride option); pavement ticket machines at most or all stops plus a plethora of retail sales outlets became the norm. Oh, and Penalty Fares of course – but at a realistic level to create the "fear factor" as well as making it worth collecting.

So, having spent a considerable part of my life – both personally and professionally – getting to know how public transport works in other countries and, crucially, travelling on it extensively, I have long been convinced that the UK model needs improvement in a number of ways. The passionate adherence to the double-decker is almost uniquely British and certainly London-ish, and those of us involved in one way or another in bringing articulated buses to the capital were convinced they had a lot to offer in comparison with the traditional approach - once again, study tours with key London Buses people to several German and Swiss cities underlined their significant advantages. From my point of view, as the champion of accessibility, the attractions of a bus with all the seats on one level and space to avoid most pinch points for wheelchair-users and parents with buggies was well worth investigating.

It soon became clear that these "people movers" were ideal for the heavily-peaked "Red Arrow" routes (on which, at the very least, they should have been retained) and that they could achieve better stop dwell times than crew-operated RMs. This was, of course, a result of the "open boarding" policy necessitated by the introduction of three-door 18-metre vehicles though this famously (but unintentionally on TfL's part) became the fulcrum of the relentless *Evening Standard* campaign to convince the world that no passenger ever paid a fare on a "bendybus" (awful word, by the way)!

At the time (and the proportion was significantly falling, eventually to zero with on-bus sales withdrawn completely), only a very small number of passengers were paying in cash and the Oyster Card – mostly loaded with a Travelcard product or Bus Pass – already represented by far the ticket of choice. I have to say (partly in hindsight) that this was perhaps the "Achilles Heel" of the whole project as it meant most passengers needed to do nothing on boarding an artic at any door. Hence the *Standard*'s belief that nobody paid! It should have been a mandatory requirement for Oyster Cards of all types to be validated on boarding (with the advantage of more statistical information relating to the routes concerned) and it would have been pretty easy to devise a weekly cash prize draw or similar inducement to ensure that people did.

But, in reality, what this bold move demonstrated

above all is that on some of the busiest routes in London substantial savings in costs could be achieved through the reduced peak vehicle requirement compared to double-deckers – amply underlined by the extra 144 buses required for re-conversion of all the routes affected. Significant increases in capacity were achieved too. More importantly, from the passengers' point of view, there was a huge benefit in being able to get on the first bus to come along. Rather like Tube travel in peak hours, the choice was yours (to squeeze on board or wait for the next one) and it was an absolute joy to see the transformation of the lengthy queues at Waterloo Station from slowly shuffling forward to finally get on the 4th or 5th Leyland National to the new dawn of an 18-metre Citaro opening its doors to hoover-up the whole line!

There will, of course, be debates *ad nauseam* about the suitability of London's streets for 18-metre vehicles but they were just as easily (if not more easily) manoeuvred round tight left turns as the current generation of longer-wheelbase double-deckers (not least the Borismaster) as their drivers would attest. What was not always got right (though sometimes, rather annoyingly, it followed the removal of the artics) was the re-design of certain stops and the creation of better bus priorities – the classic examples on route 38 being the contra-flow system in Holborn and the "cut through" from Shaftesbury Avenue to Piccadilly. Measures of this sort would be second nature if trams were being introduced and the articulated bus should have been afforded similar consideration.

I spent many hours marvelling at the efficiency of the Citaro fleet and it really felt as though buses had finally come into the 21st century with the disappearance of that interminable delay at each stop as alighting passengers slowly emerged down the stairs and those boarding filed past the driver and through the "throat" to find there was little choice but to climb to the upper saloon. Whether two or thirty-two passengers were waiting at a stop, the dwell time with an artic was the same, and for the increasing numbers of older people the availability of all the seats on the "ground floor"" (rather than fewer than a third of them) made a big difference. That consistency of dwell time made a substantial contribution to improved regularity on the services concerned, and though "bunching" was not eliminated – thanks to the city's overall traffic congestion – it was certainly reduced (though I believe some operators did a better job of regulating their routes than others by carefully understanding the nature of the beast that is an articulated bus).

But life can sometimes be short and as someone once said, politics is the art of the possible which I guess was amply demonstrated by the enforcement of Mayor Johnson's manifesto pledge to rid London of what he claimed were vehicles that belonged in Scandinavian airports. Sad to say, with TfL as a personal fiefdom, these wonderful buses were bound to go – and quickly. That level of control also implies "at any cost" and it has been very costly indeed. A wasted investment *sans pareil* with almost 400 vehicles withdrawn after barely half of their working lives.

On a trip along the Uxbridge Road on the last night of Citaros on the 207, I was in the company of a very senior TfL official who cannot be named for obvious reasons but I leave you with his comment as we collected a full load in a matter of seconds: "These buses are a good idea, Andrew – someone should tell the Mayor"!

Mercedes-Benz Citaro articulated bus heads through Camden Town on route 29. Arriva eventually had the largest fleet of these vehicles for the 38, 73 and 149 in addition to the 29.

15 THE VOICE OF THE BUS
Emma Hignett

I originally trained as a dancer. I went to ballet school from 15 for three years. At some point in my third year, I had a conversation with my father. I planned to be on the stage, but out of the blue he said he could see me one day as a newsreader on the TV, and I guess this memory just stuck. I danced for a few years. Then I decided that it wasn't really the challenge I wanted, plus I was working overseas and I didn't want to be travelling so much. And, I remembered what my father had said about reading the news.

So, the next question was 'how do I get into television'? I thought via radio was the best route. At that point, I was not a big radio fan - but I started by doing radio traffic reports, and I fell in love with radio and continued working in radio for the next 15 years.

The voice-overs started as a sideline. I would be asked if I could do an advert; it wasn't something I gave a lot of attention to, it was just a nice little sideline.

Then, in my mid-30s, when I was co-hosting the breakfast show on Capital Gold in London, I decided that I was going to look for a role that that was lower profile – I'd been presenting breakfast shows at that point for about five years. I wanted to get out of London too, so I took a job running a radio station in the north-east of England. At the time I was going through the interviews, a colleague said they were putting together sample voice tapes for Transport for London's new iBus scheme and would I like to put a voice test in. A few months later I heard that I was the favourite. They'd whittled the voices down to two - it was between one male voiceover and myself.

We both recorded route 149, and they selected my voice to test on the buses in January 2006. They researched the impact of the system, and sought feedback from passengers, drivers and specific community groups such as blind travellers.

The original iBus recording sessions at Trident Studios in Soho. I have a 'buses' voice – I generally don't use my natural speaking voice when doing any voiceovers. Whenever I am in front of a microphone I just seem to speak differently.

Some of the feedback was really amusing. One driver reported that all the children on the bus who had previously made a lot of noise now spent the journeys imitating my announcements, making them far more manageable.

The original recordings were made in Trident Studios in Soho, later for a while we recorded at Palestra, the Transport for London building opposite Southwark station. I remember taking the bus there from King's Cross and literally scribbling a note of all the announcements I wasn't happy with, so that I could then re-record them! I'm more used to hearing the announcements now. When I did the first recordings, I had no idea how they'd sound, but now I travel by bus whenever I'm in London so I'm much more used to the sound.

The announcements are broken down for the recordings so I record separately stop names, route numbers, and destinations. I think we're all responsible for checking pronunciations, though the bus drivers are, I think, often the ones who can confirm for us. There is, however, one London name which is never agreed on, and that is Lido. I recorded originally 'lee-doh' and we received quite a lot of complaints. So I re-recorded as 'lie-doh' ... and we got just as many complaints!

Originally we started with 20,000 recordings to be supplied, they were recorded 2,000 at a time once a fortnight. However, I reckon we've now recorded well over 60,000 announcements in total. As I now have my own studio, I can record announcements when they're needed – whether they need a couple of hundred updates, or just one or two.

I had a funny conversation with a member of the TfL press team on the day we launched the test on the Route 149. She asked me if I knew why they had chosen my voice, and then revealed it was because ... she paused ... it was 'bland'. Maybe the wrong choice of word, but what they were looking for was a voice that wasn't going to wind people up, one that could blend a little into the background, but was there if you needed to follow the announcements. An unusual sounding voice might grate after several years ... an unusual twist to a voice is ideal if it's an advert for Asda, for example, but you don't want it on a 70-minute bus journey, day in day out. My voice is fairly straightforward, and as it happened it was what they wanted for this job - it's all about the right voice for the right job.

In 2014 there was the Year of the Bus, with various projects and celebrations including a big display of buses in Regent Street on a beautiful sunny Sunday. At the invitation of Leon Daniels, MD of TfL's Surface Transport, I had arranged to come for an hour or so to sit on the first bus, nearest to Oxford Circus, and there I'd make recordings for people, generally on their mobile phones. We thought we might get a handful of people – but we were inundated, in the end we had

to stop more people joining the queue. It showed the passion people have for London buses. I was asked to record all sorts of things. People wanted the name of the road where they lived, one asked for 'please move to your side of the bed', some wanted answerphone messages, and I even had one marriage proposal (to record)!

More recently I've recorded the announcements for the new Elizabeth Line trains as well as two other bus companies, one in the North East and one in Yorkshire. I've recently worked on a Dorling Kindersley audiobook on space travel and added my voices to a range of talking watches. I provide voiceovers for lots of different companies, but also lovers of London buses have found me via social media or my website, emmahignett.com, for their own projects. I've done answerphone messages and personal announcements. I've even done several hundred announcements for someone's model railway.

Here I am at the launch of the route 149 on-board announcements in 2006.

During the Year of the Bus Cavalcade in Regent Street – taking a rare break to try out the driver's seat.

16 THE 2012 OLYMPIC AND PARALYMPIC GAMES

Stephen Walker, Andy Thompson and John Barry

Being named host city for the Olympic Games in 2005 was a great honour for London and the country but with it came the enormous task of delivering a successful Games under the glare of the world's media. London's focus on legacy also required success to extend into the following years, long after the Olympic flame passed on to Rio. The consensus prior to 2012 was that transport could be London's Achilles heel. This is the story of how buses made their own distinctive contribution to the transport achievements of London 2012.

Three agencies were responsible for Games bus services and associated infrastructure: The London Organising Committee for the Olympic and Paralympic Games (LOCOG) ,the Olympic Delivery Authority (ODA) and Transport for London (TfL). They worked with the bus operating industry and the London Boroughs to deliver the plans.

A Games Transport Board met regularly to co-ordinate and direct activities. The allocation of responsibilities evolved as the Games approached and the post-Games legacy was built into planning from an early stage.

Going into Games Year, the London bus network was (and still remains) the most-used form of public transport in the capital and catered for 2.34 billion passenger trips in the year to April 2012. It is the only public transport mode serving every part of the city, with around 95% of Londoners living within 400 metres of a stop – around five minutes at average walking speed.

TfL's bus network therefore needed to continue functioning effectively across the city while the venues were built and during the events themselves. It was well-known that the Games would have a hugely significant impact on the road network, firstly as land and roads were acquired to build the Olympic Park from 2007 and then at Games time with special priority lanes, road closures around venues, and on-street events such as the Marathon and cycling. The "Olympic Route Network" of roads to be used by athletes and officials added up to 175km of road, with priority lanes on 48km of these. There was a similar Paralympic Route Network at a smaller scale.

Early planning and modelling showed that hosting a successful Games needed specific extra capacity on the transport networks and careful mitigation of any disruptive effects on services. TfL and its partners therefore brought forward not only capacity projects but also an innovative programme of communications asking people to reduce or retime their travel to lessen strain on the system. This was activated well before the Games and then throughout the events themselves.

The ODA acquired the land needed for the Olympic Park in July 2007 and several roads were closed. Three bus garages required permanent relocation as they lay within the site. Stagecoach's Waterden Road base (code WA) closed in 2007, the allocation for route 25 being transferred temporarily to Rainham. The former Bow midibus base, then known as Stratford (SD), closed in 2008. Stagecoach transferred to the new West Ham (WH) site provided by TfL on land vacated by Parcelforce. Operations from First's garage in Waterden Road (H) transferred to Lea Interchange (LI) just off Ruckholt Road, including hydrogen refuelling equipment for the experimental buses then in use on route RV1. As work built up, the contractors building the Olympic Park venues introduced dedicated shuttle buses for workers from Stratford.

Within the Games period there were three distinct segments, one for each of the Games and an intervening Transition period. The Opening and Closing Ceremonies for the Olympic Games were on 27 July and 12 August respectively. Corresponding dates for the Paralympics were 29 August and 9 September.

Prioritisation of Games Family movement on the Olympic Route Network commenced as athletes and officials began to arrive in London. Expanded security and spectator zones at venues were also introduced, requiring further bus diversions particularly at Whitehall, Woolwich Common, Earls Court, Wembley and Wimbledon. Passengers were kept informed through maps and other information posted online and on the network. A special sign was used to indicate bus stops with services affected by Games-time changes.

Special bus stop signage.

Route 132 (North Greenwich-Bexleyheath) was converted to double-deck.

Capacity increases also started to be implemented. Each route had bespoke variations according to expected demand, taking account of competition schedules. Some of the changes catered for general increases in travel expected at key interchanges such as London Bridge and Kings Cross St Pancras and for visitors to concerts and big-screen events laid on in Hyde Park.

The scale of bus network interventions were considerable with a total of 82 routes having some change during the Games summer. That represented around 12% of all TfL routes, carrying approximately one-fifth of TfL's bus passengers.

Costs for each change were negotiated by TfL's tendering team. Operators found the vehicles needed for enhancements and diversions in various ways, including management of their normal vehicle renewal cycle and reallocations enabled by summer schedules. TfL, LOCOG and the operators kept an overview of the combined impact of resourcing both public transport and Games Family requirements at the same time. In a small number of cases when these options were not available, frequency reductions allowed for the same number of buses to operate along extended diversionary routes.

Additionally, a small number of routes were converted to use larger buses without any changes to alignment or frequency. One such, route 132 between Bexleyheath and North Greenwich, retained its larger buses permanently. The new night service on route 238 (Stratford-Barking) also became an ongoing part of the network.

Buses carried all the normal TfL ticketing and information systems, except in a small number of cases where it was necessary to use temporary equipment. Standard fares were charged including acceptance of the Games Travelcard provided for each event ticketholder.

Further diversions and curtailments were put in place on the days of the road events. The biggest single impact arose from the cycling road races on 28 and 29 July covering a wide area of the city from the centre via the southwestern suburbs and into Surrey. A total of 67 routes were affected, some suspended entirely (routes 14, 22, 33, 74, 337, 411, 465, 481, C3 and R68) and 51 shortened. Unusual turning places included Knightsbridge Barracks for routes 9, 49, 52 and 452 and the little-used Priests Bridge stand at Sheen for route 493. The Triathlon cycling on 2, 4 and 7 August took place over a course between Buckingham Palace and Kensington Gardens via Hyde Park Corner. Many routes were diverted via the underpass and some routes

Standby buses stabled near North Greenwich.

used Pont Street and Grosvenor Square. Each of the diversions and turns required extensive preparatory work by TfL's Bus Operations team to check widths, alignments and stopping places and to secure access permissions where necessary.

TfL organised a fleet of contingency buses for use as required, for example if there were demand surges or temporary disruptions on other modes. The fleet included some vehicles from Dial-a-Ride. They were deployed on several occasions, particularly along busy corridors into Stratford. Many were based near North Greenwich, which is served directly by only a single rail line. Articulated buses were available and able to operate through the low-headroom Blackwall Tunnel. Special stabling was leased at industrial sites.

Controllers of the contingency buses aimed to anticipate potential problems so they could act with speed. Mostly this paid off, with issues averted but on a few occasions the fleet was put into action for an issue which then vanished. One on occasion there was increasing concern throughout the day about an Olympic football match held at Cardiff going into extra time and reports of an extremely busy train due to arrive in Paddington after the tube had closed. The fleet was deployed only to find a trickle of spectators emerge from the train. Apparently one lucky fan got a personal service home on one of the double deckers ....

During the Games, operational performance was reviewed at various times each day in senior management conference calls organised by TfL's

5.   OTHER

Feedback from Public/Colleagues/Other

1530 PM Briefing
- Contingency buses deployed on Central Line
- Contingency buses to be used on 108 from circa 1800

0900 Bus Operations Conference Call
- Stratford Bus station coped at egress from the Olympic Park on Friday night (circa 2200)
- Euston – 188s early running
- Routes 9 & 10 suffering delays at Hammersmith
- Security Gates broke at North Greenwich bus station causing some operational problems.
- Delays on 108s due to high loadings caused capacity problems. 2 artics deployed from contingency fleet at 0400.
- DaR – no deployment
- Triathlon today. Things have gone well so far. Roads may re-open sooner than planned.
- Possible War on Want demo
- Boris & Wiggo expected to cycle from Hyde Park to Oxford Street around 1600. May cause delays.

1100 Bus Operators Conference Call
Yesterday Friday 3 August
- Knightsbridge 45 min delays
- Savoy Circus – delays
- Gower St / Holborn delays around 1800. 521 impacted.
- Oxford Street / Haymarket / Trafalgar Square – delays.
- Wimbledon delays – affected routes 57 and 131
- Tower Bridge / Creek Road delays affected route 188

TfL Buses Games Time Data Report for 3 August 2012. (TfL)

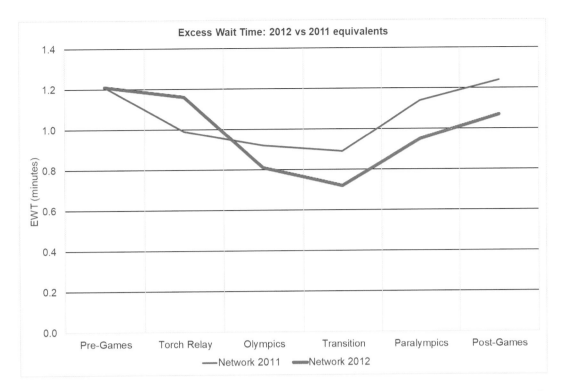

CentreComm. A report was issued each morning reviewing public and operator feedback alongside information on mileage, patronage, data collected by the CentreComm controllers, and places where the contingency buses had been used. Special loadings surveys were organised and TfL's Technical Services Group developed a new report based on downloads of vehicle location data from buses to highlight any disruption.

One of the authors was fortunate enough to have a ticket to the Paralympic Opening ceremony, a spectacular event featuring his fellow Boltonians Sir Philip Craven (President of the International Paralympic Committee) and Sir Ian McKellen (Gandalf). However enjoyment was tempered as the event ran later and later, with concerns the tube would stop before all of the crowd could reach the station. The decision was taken to deploy the contingency fleet to support the Underground and the author's night off became another working day.

Despite these large and constantly varying changes to the operating environment and service patterns, the network's patronage and reliability was maintained and even improved during the summer of 2012. The exception was the pre-Games "Torch Relay" period, which saw larger-than-expected crowds, with road closures often at relatively short notice. Apart from the careful planning of schedules and operations, bus reliability also benefited from the success of the travel demand management programme which helped rebalance pressures on the roads. In addition, after the opening weekend it was possible to reduce the proportion of Games Lanes active on any given day during the Olympics to a maximum of about 40%.

Overall, during the Olympic Games around 6.5 million passengers per weekday were carried on the bus network in total, compared with under 6 million in the equivalent weeks of 2011 though these were affected by the civil disturbances that year. Around 7.5 million passengers were carried per weekday during the Paralympics, similar to the level in 2011.

Bus services to support the transformation of the Olympic site into permanent employment, leisure and other uses were incorporated into the earliest planning. Some were implemented temporarily on the opening of the Westfield retail centre in late 2011, with 22.5 buses per hour at peak times on four routes serving the new Stratford City bus station:

* Route 97 (Chingford-Leyton) extended and frequency increased to 7.5 buses per hour.
* Route 241 (Canning Town-Stratford) extended via Leyton Road.
* Route 339 (Shadwell-Fish Island) extended via Warton Road.
* Route D8 (Crossharbour-Stratford) diverted to Stratford City via Warton Road.

These services were curtailed during the Games then reinstated in 2013 and 2014, some in revised form. New services via the centre of the Park were added. TfL's proposals were drawn up after planning work with the London Legacy Development Corporation and the local boroughs. They were implemented with some amendments and further changes have since occurred.

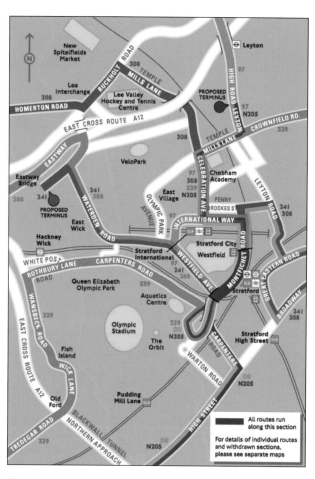

In parallel with the work on TfL bus services, an integral part of the successful bid to host the London 2012 Games was the provision of dedicated Games Family Transport bus and coach services for athletes, accredited media and technical officials (umpires, referees, etc).

LOCOG was responsible for the delivery of Games Family Transport services in accordance with established standards developed and refined over successive summer and winter games by the International Olympic Committee (IOC). Their purpose is to provide secure, rapid and reliable transport links between accommodation and training and competition venues both pre-, during and post-Olympic and Paralympic games periods. In addition, services were provided between the main ports of entry such as Heathrow and accommodation and to and from opening and closing ceremonies for both Games.

The IOC standards specify separate networks of point-to-point services for each of the three Games Family client groups operating from early morning to late night between all relevant accommodation locations and all competition and training venues. These services are required to operate at pre-set frequencies, with the capability of providing duplicate journeys to boost capacity as required to meet fluctuations in demand. Similar but differing networks were designed for both the Olympic and Paralympic Games.

Above: Service changes proposed for the re-opening of the Olympic Park post-Games.

Below: Media bus at Russell Square Media Mall.

Facing page: Athlete buses at Olympic Village Athlete Bus Mall.

Accommodation

Athletes

Olympic Village within the Olympic Park – 'Athlete Mall' created next to Olympic Village

Media

Multiple hotel locations around London – 'Media Mall' created at Russell Square as a focal point

Technical officials

Multiple hotel locations generally close to relevant competition venues

Competition venues

Olympic Park (multiple venues), Excel Centre, North Greenwich Arena, Greenwich Park, Royal Artillery Barracks, Horse Guards Parade, Hyde Park, Earls Court, Lords, Wimbledon, Wembley

Training venues

Competition venues plus other facilities throughout London

The combined scale of these networks was considerable with approximate peak bus and coach vehicle requirements of 400, 600 and 150 for athletes, media and technical officials respectively. Reflecting the separate networks created for each Games Family client group, separate dedicated bus stop arrangements were created at each origin and destination for each service type.

As part of the LOCOG organisational structure, a Transport Team progressively expanded as summer 2012 approached. This was staffed by a mixture of local and international colleagues with a variety of previous experience, including games and major events, transport authority and operators. Included in this mix was a small team seconded from TfL to lead the procurement of vehicles and drivers, scheduling, depot design and

Buses parked in temporary depot at Royal Albert Dock with driver accommodation cruise ship moored alongside.

Games time operation of services. One author was the first to be seconded from 2009. This was early enough to allow a working visit to Vancouver during the 2010 Winter Games to gain a valuable insight into the IOC games operations model.

There were some well-known faces behind the scenes. The author remembers being asked early in his secondment to drop into a meeting and update on progress to find Seb Coe at the head of the table. LOCOG luminaries Jonathan Edwards, Tim Henman, Tanni-Grey Thompson and Ade Adepitan were all regulars at the office.

As an early part of the procurement process, Stagecoach was appointed as a lead operator to assist with scheduling, training, and depot operations. To ensure enough supply to meet the considerable requirement for buses, coaches and drivers, extensive industry engagement took place during 2010 covering all nations and regions of the UK and Ireland. This proved successful and approximately 60 bus and coach operators were awarded supply contracts in numbers ranging from under 10 to hundreds of vehicles during

summer 2012. To accommodate this scale of operation, two large temporary bus depots were created on sites owned by the London Development Agency:

* A highly secure 400-capacity depot was established for vehicles and drivers providing the Athlete services in West Ham. This was on the remainder of the former Parcelforce site behind the new WH facility occupied by Stagecoach.

* A vast 600-capacity depot located adjacent to Royal Albert Dock opposite City Airport. This was the base for the vehicles and drivers providing the services for the Media and Technical Officials. As well as its geographical convenience, a key advantage of this site was that it enabled a cruise ship used to accommodate 800 drivers to be moored immediately alongside.

Both depots had full vehicle washing and fuelling facilities provided by games sponsor BP, as well as temporary maintenance, office, and canteen facilities. During the Games, drivers were visited at the temporary depots by Eddie Izzard in his role as an ambassador to frontline staff.

Following the three-year period of planning, procurement, depot construction, scheduling, test events and preparation, the major challenge of mobilisation commenced from June 2012. This involved the 'on-boarding' of nearly 3,000 drivers and over 1,000 buses and coaches. Drivers underwent final security accreditation, training, including route learning and depot and venue familiarisation. Vehicles were delivered to the temporary depots, inspected and equipped with radios, satnav equipment and a large sticker identifying them as part of the Games Family fleet to assist with camera enforcement of the Olympic Route Network lanes. Temporary licensing arrangements had been put in place in advance through close collaboration with the Traffic Commissioners for Great Britain. Most drivers were not local and required accommodation which was provided in student facilities and on the cruise ship referred to above.

Operation of the first services commenced on 1st July 2012, built to a peak during the live Olympic Games period between 27th July and 12th August, continued through the transition period between the Olympic and Paralympic Games and peaked again during the Paralympic Games from 29th August to 9th September, finally ending by late September.

Throughout the operation, depot-based dispatch and service control teams worked closely with frontline venue and athlete and Media Mall colleagues, the majority of whom were volunteer 'Games Makers', to ensure that all services were delivered in accordance with the exacting standards of the three Games Family client groups. There was also close and continuous communication with the Olympic Control Centre and CentreComm. The teams were particularly stretched on the days of the opening and closing ceremonies of both Games when, as well as the daily service requirements,

General view of temporary bus depot at Royal Albert Dock.

Driver console housing radio and satnav.

significant additional services were provided to support these major events.

As part of the training, all staff and volunteers were guided to act professionally and give athletes and other famous faces space and not to disturb their focus by asking for selfies. Usain Bolt, the 100 metres champion from Jamaica was often seen using the athlete buses and attracted a lot of positive feedback from Games Makers as he went out of his way to show his appreciation. This included spontaneously adopting his signature victory pose for pictures while boarding!

During the two-week transition period between the Olympic and Paralympic Games, the Transport Team faced the challenge of converting the interior layout of approximately 300 single-deck buses into a Paralympic athlete configuration. This was a carefully planned operation that required close collaboration with the certifying agency VOSA and vehicle manufacturers ADL and Wrights to achieve type approval of temporary vehicle layouts. These were designed to maximise capacity for wheelchair users and involved the removal of seating and installation of equipment to create an

additional 4-5 wheelchair spaces. This was a first in Paralympic Games transport history. During the Games transition period, a vehicle conversion production line was set up in Stagecoach's mothballed former garage at Upton Park supported by Games sponsor UPS. This facility was also used following the Games to restore the buses to their original specifications.

Following the conclusion of the service delivery period, drivers and vehicles were repatriated to their home depots, temporary depots were decommissioned, and the Transport Team was progressively disbanded. After a long, intense, and successful operation, this had been an unforgettable experience!

The general verdict, both nationally and internationally, was that the 2012 Olympic and Paralympic Games were a great success. The fear that transport might not cope proved unfounded. Buses played their role in that success by moving the Games Family, spectators and, not least, Londoners going about their daily business. After the Games the network adapted to support transformation in Stratford and the Olympic Park and that legacy continues to this day.

Above: Paralympic conversion completed.

Below right: Special pink signs supplemented existing signage to assist the efficient movement of visitors.

Below: A special network of road priority routes was in place for Olympic and Paralympic traffic.

17 THE RISE AND FALL OF A PHOENIX
Doug Rose

Extracts from the last bus map by Ben Lewis (above) and the first by David Penrose (below), both reproduced here at the size they were printed for the pocket folder.

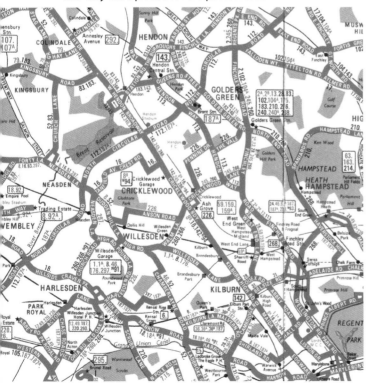

The London General Omnibus Company issued its first bus map in 1910, with bus route numbers appended in numerical order alongside the roads served. Though other styles briefly came and went along the way, this presentation lasted pretty much unchallenged until the early 1980s. That decade then saw a radical change in London Transport's approach to its bus maps, and the 1990s saw a rebellion against it from within. This is the story of what happened.

Setting the scene

I joined FWT in July 1979 as assistant to David Penrose, who had joined this fledgling company from Cook Hammond & Kell (CH&K) in May. It was just the two of us in those much simpler days, before procurement departments assumed power over managers with subject knowledge and a sound and trusting relationship with reliable suppliers.

David had left CH&K, who were based in Mitcham, as a result of London Transport (LT) wanting David to work in its offices at Griffith House. This was impractical and so, with CH&K's blessing, David moved much closer to them at FWT in Moorgate. David, as CH&K's transport cartographer, had been supplier to FWT for a while too.

Frank Mussett was the man in charge of the bus map at the Publicity Office of LT and he had been working with David for many years. With David's move in place Frank still of course worked with him. I suppose I only got my job because of that.

David had drawn a new bus map which first appeared in 1969. This was a complete re-design, based on his own original design from the earlier central London tourist map. The Penrose map differed from Ben Lewis's in a fundamental way, and one that still divides opinion.

The Lewis map had quite thin lines with road names on one side and route numbers usually on the other. David Penrose's approach was for much thicker roads, with their names reversed out within, thus permitting numbers on either side. Though this gave a somewhat heavier look to the map, in my opinion the Penrose style succeeds in that it provides more flexibility in positioning route numbers on either side, in congested areas, and takes up a similar amount of space overall. More importantly, I believe the routes are easier to follow — a fundamental requirement of any bus map.

I do not know on what basis Ben Lewis's map was created, but it was not to accurate scale as can be seen when comparing road configurations with the new

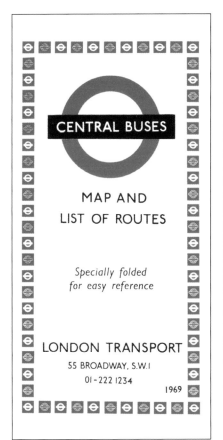

At three-quarter size, from left to right, covers of the last Ben Lewis map of 1969, the first Penrose map, also of 1969, and the first issue of the 1977 Penrose map. The earliest of these was probably the most elegant.

As might be obvious from the covers, the 1977 map opened out to a larger sheet size, though the scale was actually slightly smaller as a greater area was covered. A similar area of extract is shown below.

Penrose map, which was based on Ordnance Survey mapping. The royalties being incurred by LT on this became prohibitively expensive and David drew another new map, first issued in 1977, based on out of copyright source material.

New ideas
Michael Levey was Publicity Officer at the time and a design proposal was received from Ben Beverage to 'Undergroundize' the bus map; this found sufficient favour to be considered. Not for the first time, the existing map's usability and ability to promote London's bus services was questioned. Also not for the first time, the perennial question was asked why the Underground map was seen as such a success, whereas the bus map was not, even though no hard evidence for this ever seems to have been produced. Solution: make a bus map like an Underground map.

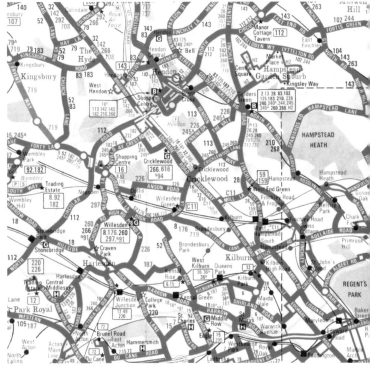

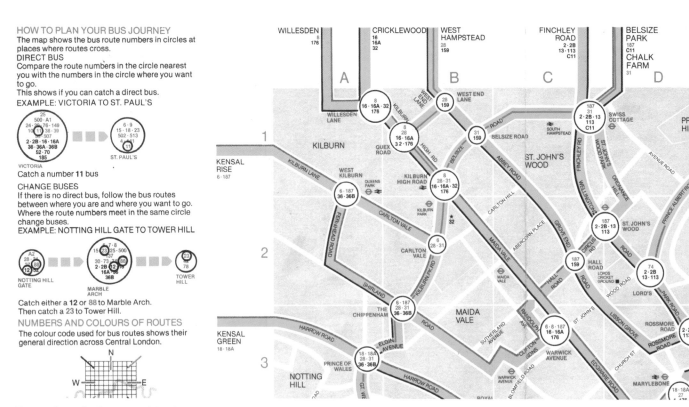

Extract from the first central London Holmes map. There are too many shortcomings of the design to go into here, but the major one was that where three roads formed a triangle and a bus route served all three, it was impossible to know which way it went – see route 6. This is a big problem as buses stop along roads and not at junctions; passengers would not know where their bus stop might be. The solution later adopted was to only add numbers alongside the roads to clarify where there was ambiguity and thus removing any argument against the Lewis/Penrose approach. This supposed solution also violated the most important rule of information design: do not portray one feature two different ways, and do not portray two different features the same as each other. (Just to be clear, David and I had nothing to do with the creation of this.)

Sadly this well-meaning but naive thinking will always fail, though it has never deterred people from trying. This raises the question: what have the two modes of transport in common? Answer: actually very little, other than the passenger has to pay before commencing any journey, and someone else does the driving. The most obvious things bus and rail do not have in common are:

- trains run within their own fixed, easily identified infrastructure, and do not have to vie for attention among the street clutter and multitude of other vehicles;
- trains have their own signage, usually kept away from the visual noise of their surroundings;
- most importantly, there are a handful of individually identifiable Underground lines (albeit some having a few service pattern variations) but there are hundreds of bus routes.

Attempts have been made in the past to colour code bus routes and others to give them complicated prefix and suffix letters, but one cannot get away from the fact that bus routes are far more complex to explain than Underground lines, and they also change far more often than a railway route ever can.

Furthermore, there are fewer than 300 stations on the Underground and about 19,000 of their equivalent on the bus network — the humble bus stop.

Unsurprisingly, research conducted in the summer of 1979 (source now unidentified) comparing the Beveridge diagram with the Penrose map, found that many people did indeed find the Penrose map difficult to use, but the majority found *any* map difficult to use — hardly a revelation worthy of the effort to establish. It was from this background that yet another attempt to create an understandable bus map was born.

The introduction to the public of the eight operational bus districts in 1979 could arguably be regarded as the first step along the way. If we disregard the central area tourist bus maps, until then there was a single bus map covering the whole of London and necessarily quite small in scale.

Seven new local maps were to be prepared from the artwork of the overall map, one for each of the six suburban districts; there was also a central area map encompassing Abbey and Tower districts from the separate central London Penrose map. The smaller catchments allowed a larger scale*. In the event only three got published: Cardinal, Forest and Watling.

A new design emerges

By late 1979 a small group within LT, headed by Roger Graef, set about commissioning design research, though curiously, bearing in mind his decades of experience and subject knowledge, David Penrose was not among them — perhaps being seen as a supplier and so not totally impartial.

In the space available here I cannot go into the various design ideas that emerged and will instead concentrate on the outcome. That said, architect/artist Andrew Holmes was brought into the design group by Roger Graef and his solution was implemented in many forms.†

After some experimentation, and almost by accident according to some commentators, Holmes came up with a radical new approach. He dispensed altogether with route numbers alongside the roads and instead introduced circles at bus road junctions and heaped the numbers within those. His rationale was that this made working out where to change bus much easier — perhaps it did but the disadvantages of this appeared to outweigh any benefit.

LT went back to David's previous employer Cook Hammond & Kell — the company being of justifiably high repute as cartographers with a history dating from 1860. Unfortunately, without David, what they were not were cartographers with bus operation and the associated mapping experience. Over a long and drawn out process gradually a new all-London map was created. When it appeared in print in 1983 it was much derided as it was littered with hundreds of errors. Andrew Holmes, too, was not practised in bus operation and this combination of designer and cartographer was actually unfair on both. It also didn't give the design concept much of a chance in real life use. LT persevered.

The situation was not helped by the Penrose map having been withdrawn. LT's reaction to the fallout was to stop production of an all-London map altogether and introduce larger scale local maps in the Holmes style instead, though these had nothing to do with the earlier operating district maps.

The reaction to the new maps had to be justified it seemed and so we at FWT were asked to produce two

maps for market research. The Ealing area was chosen, perhaps because that was where the now head of the department, Nick Lewis, lived. One map would be in the Penrose style and one in Holmes, and this was actually my first encounter with Andrew Holmes. My one enduring memory of him was when he corrected my (conventional I believe) pronunciation of 'mauve' (mowv) to 'morv'.

The two maps were produced, with David doing all the editorial this time and thus increasing the accuracy hugely. We could not have given the Holmes map a fairer outing despite having little belief in a design with so many usability shortcomings.

Much to our annoyance we were dictated to as to colour scheme and some poor typeface choices. Thelma Wright, Nick Lewis's assistant, insisted we did not have red roads. She told me red meant danger and so we had to use blue. Had I been a bit older and wiser, and a bit braver, I would have asked if she was scared of pillar boxes and telephone kiosks — oh and London buses. Another important loss was the differentiation of black and red route numbers on previous Penrose maps. The former helpfully depicted routes with a full seven-days-a-week service, as opposed to red ones where this was not the case.

We also had to have a grey background on both maps, which affected the blue more damagingly than the yellow, though the latter disappeared in the then standard yellow sodium vapour street lighting. Being a cynic I would also say that I expect the outcome of the research had been decided before we printed any maps.

There is no doubt in my mind that anything other than the most carefully considered simplification of a complex network will inevitably let the user down, though this might only become evident when the map is used in real situations. We of course favoured the blue map over the yellow but could not in all honesty endorse either.

Market research

Despite my suspicions about the quality of the research to be carried out, LT did take advice from the company employed to conduct it — they referred to the maps as samples 'C' and 'L' on the premise that people might be subliminally influenced to choose 'A' over 'B'. One for the psychologists to let me know what they think.

I do not know what methods were imposed on the testing, nor by which criteria the Holmes map was chosen. However, it was then decided to produce a range of Local Guides in that style.

The local maps were borne of the internal opinion that few people made long journeys by bus, and this is as true today as it has probably always been. However, there were, and still are, people who *do* make long

---

* The concept of 'scale' is not about bigger or smaller, it is about changing content proportions at bigger or smaller scales. No more usable space is created by simply enlarging an area of mapping.

† Readers wanting a fuller exposition of other designs considered, the decisions made and ideas discarded, are directed to Mike Horne, Jonathan Roberts, Doug Rose, *Getting There: an Assessment of London Transport's Endeavour to Improve Bus Passenger Information Literature for Central London, 1979-1985*, London Passenger Transport, No.13 (May 1985) which can be found at: www.dougrose.co.uk/index_getting-there-bus-maps-1979-85.htm

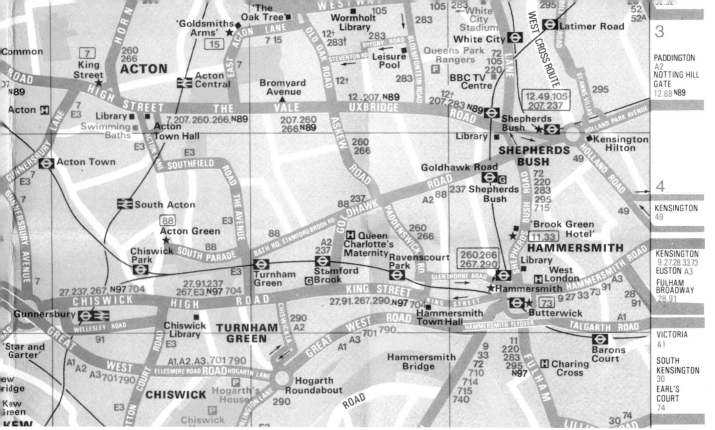

The two maps for testing. Above is the Penrose style (Map 'C') and below that from Holmes (Map 'L'). Superficially the Holmes map scores better in looking lighter on the eye and the contrast between background and roads is better – but only in ideal daylight conditions. Deeper inspection reveals that the Holmes map does not show route termini and routes seem to just disappear at Hammersmith, for example. Furthermore, the Penrose maps to date used black numbers where a full seven-days-a-week services operated and red ones where it was less so. This useful differentiation was also lost by order of LT in our brief, though the Holmes style of somewhat arbitrary directional colour coding was retained.

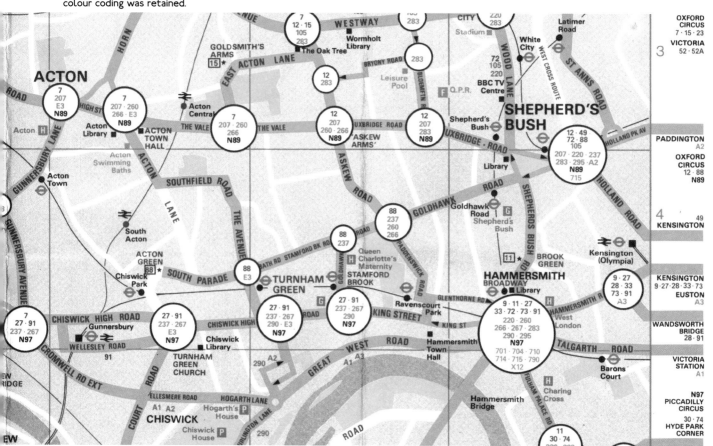

journeys by bus, often requiring one or more changes of route.

Phoenix time

Frank Mussett rang FWT one day in July 1984 to ask us to revive the Penrose map and bring it up-to-date. This was a huge job. Since last published the map had missed about five major service revisions. To give some context to the magnitude of the job it is worth explaining the methodology we used to update this map each time.

It is tempting to think that a large printed copy could have its revisions marked on it for the cartographers to work from. This won't work. Service revisions take many forms, the majority of which are:

- route numbers needing removing if re-routed or completely withdrawn;
- route numbers needing adding if re-routed or for a new route;
- route numbers changing from black to red or vice versa, according to the service quality;
- roads changing from bus served to not;
- roads changing from non-bus to bus served;
- termini moving, being removed or added;
- all manner of supporting features, such as railway stations, places of interest, facilities such as museums and hospitals changing status.

We received very little firm instruction from LT and had always taken responsibility for knowing what revisions were needed; this editorial was no small task and took up as much time as revising the map itself.

We used to go to Frank's office at least once a week to collect whatever had been put in our box on his desk. Via this we received the frequent planning meeting minutes months in advance of any proposed changes and had to track if the noted revisions changed status, month by month, which they often did. We also received proofs of new timetables as these could affect the black and red route numbers.

We were also plugged into Travel Information weekly staff bulletins, though in truth we had already carried out most of what was in them by the time they were issued a week beforehand. We had good contacts with the operating district managers and also with British Rail (station name changes sometimes occurred). We also went out of our way to monitor tourism organizations and the London boroughs in case they told us anything useful — and even the NHS for hospital information. Bearing all this in mind it is not hard to see why CH&K and Andrew Holmes struggled.

As marking the volume of revisions on a printed map was impractical, David had long since devised a much better solution. As soon as the latest printed Quad Royal poster was available, we fitted one to Sundaela board (a sort of fibreboard) and wherever a revision was needed, a numbered pin was inserted. Separately, an index was created, in numerical pin order, with each revision having its own entry. We hand-wrote this index using coloured pens that replicated the colours of the features on the map to be changed. Each pin entry had two columns, one for deletions and one for additions. We systematically ploughed our way across the map and pulled out each pin as that particular revision was done. We were ready for proof checking when there were no pins left.

This sounds complicated but wasn't and actually worked very well. The principal difficulty was wading through the source information we had accumulated since the previous update, applying the pins and writing the index. Of necessity, the process used to be almost continuous and started again as soon as the latest revision had been completed.

The real problem with this massive update we were asked to do was that we had stopped the continual analysis of the source information, though thankfully we were still receiving it from within LT; we had however stopped making our own regular contacts with those from without and had to play catch up.

The task of establishing every update was made doubly difficult as we had to analyse everything that had changed since the last printed edition. During that time, some routes had changed more than once of course and we could not simply use the latest service bulletins and minutes. This meant we could not start updating the map until all the editorial was finished, obviously affecting timescales for completion where we had been put under some pressure to do all this quickly. We had to introduce shiftwork to shorten the lead time.

The map was usually updated about three times a year but it had now been neglected for over a year. Though it obviously varied a lot, a normal revision used a couple of hundred pins and the coloured number labels we used only went up to 160. We overcame this by using different coloured numbered pin sets and seldom needed more than two. This revision took us into well over a thousand pins being required, and even finding a source of coloured pins and numbered labels to stick to the huge quantity more we needed was tricky. The revised map appeared in November 1984, though LT stubbornly retained the Holmes style map for the larger central London map on the other side — thus mixing styles and I am sure confusing a lot of people.

Psychologists are aware of a human condition which makes us not change our plans even when things go wrong and, when just stopping to re-evaluate, would result in much better decisions: it is called 'Plan Continuation Bias'. LT pressed on.

Still going round in circles

Local guides continued using the Holmes style maps, complete with all their inevitable distortions, sometimes quite grossly, to incorporate the huge junction circles at places like Croydon and Romford.

Staff reaction against the Holmes design was largely dismissed, especially of those on the front line at Travel Information offices where dealing with passengers (thankfully not yet called 'customers') was reportedly not much fun.

Undeterred LT pressed on with producing Local Guides in the Holmes style. Realizing this was no small task half were awarded to us at FWT (now a bigger company) and half to Thames Cartographic, the latter another company with no experience of bus operation: bus mapping requires a good understanding of operational practices, in order to convey them to users.

The guides had generous overlaps and this caused areas of interpretation to differ where the two suppliers' maps overlapped. At FWT we tried our hardest to make the best of a mapping system we had no faith in. Perhaps we tried too hard as we wanted make the routes as clear as possible.

In truth, this was not a particularly enjoyable period for us. Furthermore, and not that it mattered, but in those pre-computer days it also made the technical side of the job getting from artwork to press more difficult and more expensive.

Over the years the Local Guides varied a lot in quantity and coverage and continued alongside the conventional Penrose All-London map until a new regime came on the scene.

London Regional Transport rings the changes

In LT days the by now named Advertising & Publicity department (A&P) had provided a central function, as buses and Underground were regarded as one network. The creation of London Regional Transport (LRT) in 1984 presaged the eventual parting of the ways, preparatory to privatizing the operational side of the bus network. London Bus Services Ltd (hereafter referred to simply as 'Buses' and responsible for network planning and tendering) would be created as a subsidiary of LRT and, oddly, A&P was transferred to London Underground Ltd with a remit to provide services for Buses.

FWT also had a surprise coming, when A&P told us we would no longer be doing the All-London bus map, as it was being computerized by Datamap, more of which below.

With the passage of some thirty years, I am not clear on what happened but by the early 1990s Buses had waged a friendly sort of rebellion and started to take its own publicity into its own hands. This coincided with computer production just about being able to cope

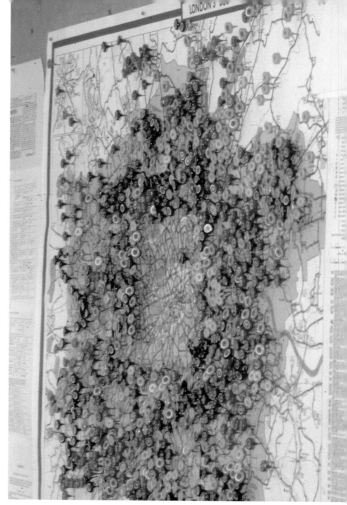

The previous edition of the Quad Royal poster to be issued, sporting the index correction pins for each update needed. By the time I took this picture some of the revisions had been done, and the associated pins removed.

with producing the Local Guides, but not the All-London (also often called 'Londonwide').

David was by now having thoughts about retirement and I was taking a much more prominent role in production management. When the call came from Buses we at FWT of course responded, though it put us in rather a piggy-in-the-middle situation with A&P.

Perhaps wanting to 'make a stand' and perhaps genuinely having the hatred for the Holmes maps they expressed, Buses wanted rid of them, but just before then a major change also took place at FWT.

Though doing well we were a small company and had made our first tentative steps into using Macintosh computers. Our relationship with CH&K was excellent and they used to do most of our pre-press work. They were much larger than us, also owning Oxford Cartographers and the retail National Map Centre. Oxford Cartographers had set up a small department within called Datamap, using (then) high end computer hardware and software. By today's standards it was so primitive that most readers will not be able to relate to the extreme limitations and complexity of its use.

There was a will from both FWT and CH&K for the latter to buy us out. FWT could provide the Macintosh expertise so needed at CH&K's own drawing office at Mitcham and FWT could benefit from the purchasing power for equipment it needed to buy. On 2nd January 1992 FWT became part of the CH&K Group and only weeks later we were asked to take over Datamap. I had no understanding of their systems and had to learn quickly. Frankly, it was crude and also enormously complex. To give a small flavour of this, outputting a single map proof took about fourteen hours of third-party supplier computer processing to create a file, that then took hours to print one copy. No 'control P' in those days.

Once again FWT had been out of the loop for the All-London map for a while. I cannot go into all the design developments that took place in the interim but it was realized that yellow roads on a grey background was not a particularly good idea; gradually the roads got darker and the background went yellow.

Thrown back into it again, as part of my learning curve I asked from what source was the map linework digitized. The Local Guides had been produced by Thames and FWT from an aerial survey commissioned by A&P to avoid paying Ordnance Survey royalties, which would have been crippling with the quantity of guides being printed.

As referred to earlier, distortions on the Holmes maps were unavoidable owing to the nature of the design, and the more complex areas could get quite 'wild'. Another major issue was that one-way systems and complex junction were routinely overwhelmed by one circle. This made using the maps to navigate in the street impossible.

It will not take a lot of imagination to understand that joining these two map sets would cause even more distortion — but that's what had been done. Datamap had then digitized over the top of this compilation. Once again client and supplier did not have the subject knowledge and the legacy of this bad decision lasted right up until the All-London's last days in 2016, but we need to step back to the early 1990s again now.

All change please

Under the leadership now of Norman Cohen, a busman through and through, Buses decided they wanted a thorough review of all passenger-facing information — everything.

I was invited to a meeting at the offices of appointed international design consultants, Fitch, where senior officers from Buses were also in attendance. From many years of encountering 'designers' I had learnt that they were (mostly) good at creating imagery but

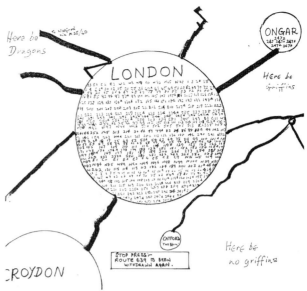

One member of Travel Information staff got very fed up with it.

hopeless at understanding manufacture and printing.

With much trepidation on my behalf the meeting commenced. There were two people from Fitch present, Graham Rhodda and Elaine Chambers. My eyebrows raised sharply and a wry smile crept across my face when I heard them ask for a free travel pass each, for bus and Underground. They had no pre-conceptions and wanted to experience the system extensively first, and would not provide suggestions, let alone designs, until they had satisfied themselves they understood the product. They also said they wanted a separate meeting with me before any products could be designed for mapping purposes, as they needed to have a grasp of the possible and in open forum made it clear they were not cartographers.

I can't remember another occasion coming out of a meeting with such high hopes — my hopes were not dashed. Graham and Elaine were a delight to work with and we became good friends.

Among the products that were created and rigorously tested by Fitch and FWT before any member of the public was let loose on them (unlike the Holmes maps) were:
- greatly improved Where to Board Your Bus panels;
- the unfortunately named 'spider' maps;
- re-designed Local Guides, mapping and supporting information;
- re-designed bus stop flags;
- re-designed service update leaflets;
- bespoke All-London map extracts for shelters;
- re-designed All-London map and supporting information.

There was a view within Fitch that any colour of bus road needed 'quietening down' and they strongly favoured grey. I didn't but lost that one. At the outset

This is from the 1994 Datamap central London map. The software used ran on a Microstation platform and used 'Image Mapper' software for output. There was no such thing for this as 'fonts' and they had to be digitized. In the mapping files line thicknesses didn't exist and nor did colour; at output stage complex links were needed to bring the linework, the fonts and the colour make-up tables together. Forget 'What You See Is What You Get'.

Readers might struggle to reconcile this map with the first Holmes map shown earlier, so much was it distorted. See also below right for what the phoenix looked like when it died again.

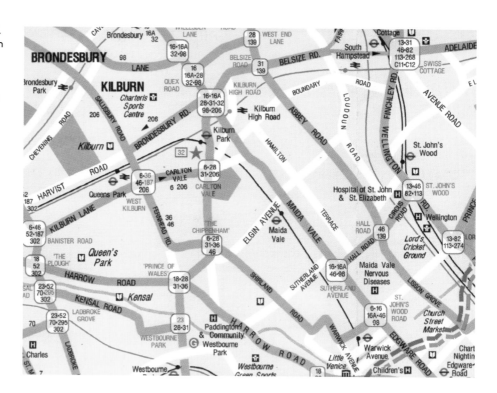

Buses wanted termini to be made much stronger, a complete contradiction to Holmes's laissez-faire attitude. The first sample proofs don't survive as far as I know but even Buses agreed what they asked for was too much; these termini were subdued quite quickly.

Everyone agreed that the All-London was a bit too small in scale and printing it any larger was impractical. London is a large area. The compromise I put forward was for four quadrant maps, with generous overlaps. This wasn't going to suit everyone but was adequate for the vast majority. The debate I lost was for the separate central London map to have a larger overlap with the outer quadrants. Routes like the 31 and 253 suffered in meandering in and out of the central London map and in and out of their overlapping quadrant map.

I explained to a now rather more attentive client the massive problems of unacceptable geographical inaccuracies we had inherited from the previous decision some years earlier. It was agreed we could fix the worst excesses but there was no appetite to do it properly and start again.

It took several months to get the map into a usable form. It would have to perform some complex tasks and the file structure was way beyond conventional graphics packages.

Each quadrant map needed to only include routes running within it and any that only ran in the overlap with a neighbouring quadrant had to be removed. The overlaps also had to have a different background tint to draw attention to them. Then things got really exciting.

For many decades a Quad Royal (40x50 inches and now 1016x1270mm) All-London poster had been provided at most bus shelters. Again, working on the principle that most people don't make long journeys by bus, it was decided we cease these and instead have a smaller area, larger scale Double Royal (40x25 inches and now 1016x635mm), bespoke to each stop. Colin Harnor from Buses (I think he had most of London's bus routes in his head) and I spent a few days working out how best to do this. Any pair of stops on opposing sides of the road would need a quite different map catchment, to best capture where each route serving would be heading.

We ended up with 53 Double Royals, plus a few based on the central London map and a special one requested by the Corporation of London. We had to work out how many bus stops would be satisfied by the appropriate map from the set. Every bus stop had to be plotted on the overall map before we could work out the extract areas. This number was needed in order to organize print quantities. In due course these posters fell out of use as the 'spider' posters gradually superseded them from around 2005, though this took many years.

As is frequently the case, once the big decisions have been made the project is handed over to lower ranking people. Subsequently everyone has an opinion how to make the map better. As soon as space is available someone will want to fill it. Bit by bit it got more and more cluttered with well-intentioned features that would help only a very few users.

The 'spider' maps have evolved since their inception, though the basic principle remains. This example is of the November 2019 edition for Victoria.

In my opinion the off-map boxes are distracting and draw too much attention relative to their worth. They were not part of the original concept.

It also disappoints me to note unexplained features on this diagram – not good practice. What are the unnamed white dots on many of the route lines? They look to the user like place names have been missed by accident. Furthermore, the temptation to be helpful and add more clutter has raised its head again, spoiling our intended simplicity at a cost to the high priority information.

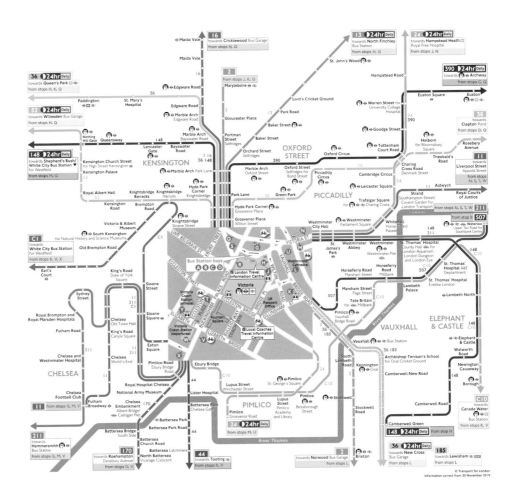

Maps like this routinely go through 'spring cleans' to de-clutter and then gradually fill up again. The Underground 'map' is another example of this for people who have studied its evolution. When the four quadrants were last issued, in 2016, it was over-burdened with supporting information.

Long before this the Marketing Department from Buses had found itself merged with A&P. In recent times Transport for London (successor to LRT in 2000) has been through several re-organizations. Very sadly most of the people with real subject knowledge were seen as a bit of a nuisance and pretty much all have gone.

The phoenix dies again

Soon after the last set of quadrants and central London bus map were printed, they were quietly dropped. This time, though there had been an outcry from some very sensible and senior people, we live in a society where most passengers are happy to be told what to do by their pocket telephone. Anyone wanting to make their own mind up what to do and where to go, and open a map and see the capital's endless travel opportunities for themselves, were sadly no longer catered for.

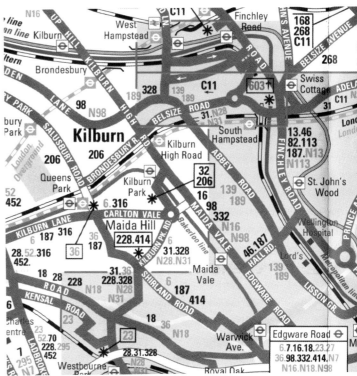

The same area, from the last edition in 2016. Again, it is hard to reconcile the geography with previous maps, and I believe too many 'good ideas' had been added.

18 THE CONTROL OF LONDON'S BUS SERVICES
Norman Cohen

I was a senior manager in London Transport's Bus Operating department during the '70s, '80s and '90s. In my first post I was responsible for researching the potential for applying radio and computer technology to bus operation. I was appointed Operations Director in the run up to privatisation of parts of the undertaking, but I kept a keen interest in developments.

"London's buses: you wait half an hour, then three turn up together". The old joke certainly applied in the 1950s and 1960s. For waiting passengers, what mattered was the long wait rather than the three at once, although that was undoubtedly an added annoyance. Why did it happen and could modern technology help? As we'll see the answer is that there were several causes, and technology has been part of the solution.

The control task is to minimise the effects of these disruptions so as to provide the best possible service for passengers. The task can be broken down into three stages:

1. Information about the location of buses
2. Deciding what action to take, if any
3. Implementing the action

The 1950s and 1960s

The only technology used to control bus services was a network of roadside telephones for the sole use of inspectors based at strategic points. Using a booklet with the scheduled times for every bus on each route passing that point, the inspector noted down the actual times (stage 1). He/she would be aware of buses already cancelled because of crew (most routes were staffed by a driver and conductor) or vehicle shortages, commonplace at the time. The inspectors used the phones to keep each other informed. Their objective (stage 2) was to even out the service, avoiding severe gaps as much as possible by instructing drivers of selected buses (stage 3) to deviate from their schedule, mainly by turning short of the scheduled terminus to fill a gap in the opposite direction, or to hold back a few minutes to even out the service. Inspectors took account of the need for crews to reach the relief point. There were also constraints on what action the inspector could take arising from agreements reached between management and the trade union. In some cases, crew behaviour (e.g. driving deliberately slowly or following the bus in front too closely) could cause gaps.

Hackney's RM 1945 passes a BESI scanner at Hyde Park Corner, which scans the plate fitted towards the front of the bus to inform central control of its position.

Of course, the inspectors' knowledge of how the service was running was limited to what they observed at the roadside. In 1958 a new system called BESI (Bus Electronic Scanning Indicator) was trialled on Route 74 (later extended to several other central London routes). It consisted of a pole at each point fitted with a light beam. Each bus on the route had a reflective plate with an identifying code attached to the side of the bus. As the bus passed a roadside pole, the light beam picked up the reflection and a signal was passed through landlines to the Fleet Communications Centre above Mansion House station (later called Centrecom). Inspectors at the centre logged each signal, thereby assisting with stage 1. The intention was that they would then decide whether action was needed to reduce a gap in service (stage 2) and if so to phone a roadside inspector to instruct the relevant bus driver (stage 3). In practice there was little improvement to the service. Some buses were not logged, but perhaps more importantly the process of information collection and subsequent decision making was too laborious.

The 1970s

A major step forward was made when buses were fitted with radios so that Centrecom was in direct contact with bus drivers. The primary purpose was to provide a means for drivers to call for assistance when there were incidents on the road such as accidents, assaults on staff, vehicle breakdowns. For the four BESI routes, there was now the added facility for Centrecom to instruct drivers directly (improving stage 3). However, surveys did not provide evidence of significant improvement in the quality of service.

Given that all buses were fitted with radio a trial was implemented in 1972 on route 76 whereby an inspector based at Centrecom maintained exclusive contact with drivers on this route. Drivers gave their location directly to the inspector (stage 1) who kept a paper log and took appropriate action to avoid gaps as much as possible (stages 2 and 3). At times drivers were prone to be inaccurate in giving their information. In the parlance of the time, the driver might "scratch for a turn": run deliberately slowly because of alleged traffic delays so that the inspector would instruct him to turn short of the full route. Even so, there was some observable improvement in the service.

A further application of radio technology was to equip roadside inspectors with pocket radios, so that they were then freed from having to stay next to the landline-based telephone. They could move to a different location on the route and still remain in contact with each other. However, they were still reliant for bus location information on direct observation of buses passing them and they still needed to speak directly to drivers. The facility was well received by inspectors, but again this wasn't reflected in the overall quality of the bus service.

An example of what we tried to avoid: three 140s together at Kenton in 1978.

Route 11 saw the introduction of a system that tackled stages 1 and 3 together by using both radio and computer technology. This was CARLA (Computer Automated Radio Location Aid). An inspector based at Centrecom was provided with a computer screen that showed the location of every bus on the route (stage 1). Buses were fitted with odometers that tracked the movement of the bus. This information was transmitted by radio to the computer which calculated the position of the bus on the route. The inspector was now free from the task of locating buses and was immediately able to see gaps forming in the service. He/she could thus attend to what action to take (stage 2) and communicate directly with drivers (stage 3). Technical issues caused some problems, especially when the computer translated the bus movement information into where it was on the route. The information needed to be calibrated by a number of microwave beacons at points along the route, triggering the bus radio to establish where the bus was. Without this addition, a bus could be travelling in a different direction or even on a different route without the computer knowing.

The system was well received by management and inspectors, but initially had a guarded response from the Trade Union, because of a fear of "the spy in the cab", implying that crews were being constantly watched for any suspected misdemeanour.

There was some reduction in gaps in service, but there was room for improvement.

Below left: A driver operates the BUSCO box in his cab.

Below right: Central control sees the position of his bus.

Opposite: A modern computer display showing HQ how the buses on a route (in this case the 38) are running.

The 1980s

Developments occurred in the 1980s that brought significant improvements to the quality of London's bus services: the schedules were reduced to a level which reflected more realistically the prevailing staff position, so that there were far fewer buses not running because of crew shortage. A programme was underway to shorten routes, which would avoid delays at one end of a long route affecting the service further along. In addition, bus manufacturers were producing more reliable vehicles than those built in the 1970s, although at the time most of the routes relevant to this discussion were operated with the popular and reliable, albeit ageing, Routemasters. The 1986 New Operating Agreement introduced substantial changes in working practices arising from an in-depth review of the agreements between management and the trade union. The cumulative effect of these developments was measurably beneficial to service reliability.

Nevertheless, there were still frequent and unpredictable disruptions arising from traffic delays. Effective control was clearly still needed. Building on previous experience and exploiting developments in both radio and computer technology, a new system was introduced on route 36. BUSCO (Bus Control) provided an inspector with a screen showing the location of every bus as it moved along the route, and radio contact with drivers. In principle this was similar to CARLA, but with better technology.

BUSCO enabled controllers to see gaps developing in the service, usually because of hold ups in traffic. The symbol for each bus was colour coded indicating for example whether it was on time or due for crew relief. Controllers could communicate directly with drivers by speech or text. So the system successfully addressed stages 1 and 3 in the control process.

An important feature of BUSCO was the positioning of the controller. With CARLA he/she was at a remote location in Centrecom; with BUSCO the control base was in a portacabin at the vehicle exit from Peckham bus garage, which was the base for route 36 and on the line of its route. The relationship between controller and crews was therefore less impersonal. The "spy in the cab" was now a recognisable person, thus restoring the direct interface that crews were used to with the teams of roadside inspectors. Stage 2 – absorbing the information presented by the system and deciding what action to take – was still up to the controller. At the time controllers were selected from the ranks of senior inspectors. They were given comprehensive training in how to use the system. Even so it became clear that some controllers were much better at doing this job than others. With more than sixty buses on the road, the controller would be presented with a considerable amount of information. It became clear that appointees to this job required special skills that could quickly absorb the information and formulate actions. In addition, it also became clear that the physical location of the controller was not as critical as had been thought. If the basics of BUSCO were to be extended to more routes, the controllers would need to be selected by recruiting people who had the required

aptitude and they would be based in purpose designed control rooms. The basis of the training programme was subsequently developed into a computer simulation of a route, CASCAID. (computer assisted service control aid). Problems that might arise were presented and possible actions demonstrated.

The 1990s and beyond

The experience gained by LT was put on hold for a while as the operation of buses became the responsibility of private companies providing bus services on contract to LT's successor (eventually called TfL). Perhaps the most important development in technology applicable to bus control was GPS. The location of buses could be tracked accurately and reliably by satellites with the information relayed to computers with substantially increased capacity. Bus operators established control rooms where many routes could be controlled by teams of controllers. The screen displays had added features such as the use of colour coding as with BUSCO but enhanced by exploiting the capabilities of computer advancements. Several routes could be controlled from each control desk by enabling the controller to switch between routes. In time all routes, both high and low frequency, could be controlled from control centres at various locations throughout London.

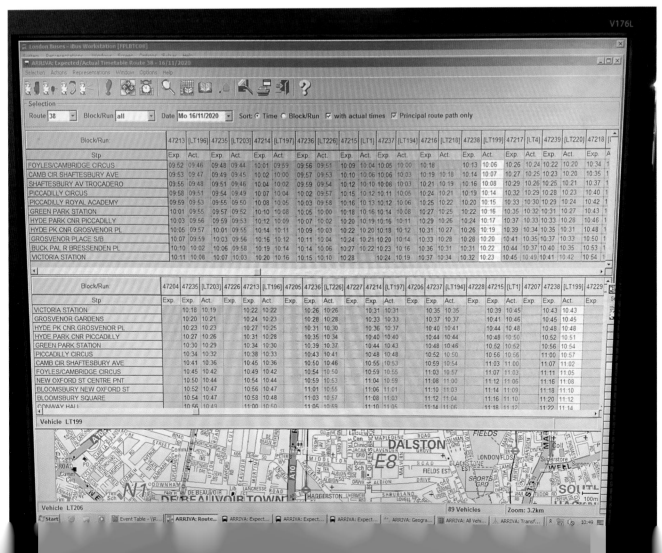

Earlier experience now led operators to recruit controllers by selecting people with the appropriate aptitudes in terms of information handling. In addition good inter-personal skills were necessary to ensure confidence and trust between controllers and drivers.

Over the period covered here, London's bus services have improved beyond what might have been envisaged in the 1960s. Virtually full staffing, reliable buses, realistic schedules, bus lanes and sensible operating practices all made this possible. But day to day problems inevitably still occur, particularly from delays in traffic. A modern control system is essential to keeping track of these problems and minimising their effect on the service.

With computers collecting so much information, it is now possible for information to be produced showing the average waiting time for each route in as much detail as would be useful to judge its performance. The Excess waiting time is a direct measure of the extent to which a route falls short of the planned schedule. TfL now used this measure in assessing operator performance. No doubt though, the old joke about buses coming in threes persists, perhaps by people who haven't used buses for years?

Peter Batty, Commercial Director, Arriva London brings the story up to date from his own perspective of working in London on the BUSCO project in the 1980s through to his experiences today delivering a consistently high level of service quality across a fifth of London's bus routes: 'Having had the opportunity to work with both Jack and Norman in the early days of my bus career, I can certainly say that the initiatives that had been developed then provide the foundation of the systems and principles of service regulation that are in place today. The political direction of the late 1980s and through to privatisation in the mid-1990s undoubtedly slowed down progress in service control development with focus directed to cost reduction as tendering expanded. The focus on service quality was renewed from 2000 as the network expanded with initiatives under the new Mayor and recognition that service reliability was the priority for passenger growth. The tendering regime in London now applied the EWT measure to contracts in addition to mileage, to incentivise operators to turn quantity into quality! This required changes in the way we scheduled and controlled routes but the reference points were there. Two examples were the training tool – CASCAID, which we dusted off from BUSCO days and now use both for training and selection. For the latter we are now able to get the right people for a job more akin to a computer game than real time bus observation on the roadside. We invested in purpose-built control centres (updating the Peckham experience with BUSCO) to provide the facilities and information for one individual to control several bus routes remotely without the requirement for roadside staff. The outcomes are reflected in a trend of continuous improvement from many routes greater than 2 minutes EWT and a wide range of outcomes even on parallel services in 2002, to an average below 0.8 minutes in 2020. The endeavour of those back in the second half of the twentieth century who believed they could find solutions to improve service reliability has been realised.'

Below: A unit in the driver's cab gives information from HQ and, where necessary, instructions.

Below right: Mobile phone display for real time passenger information.

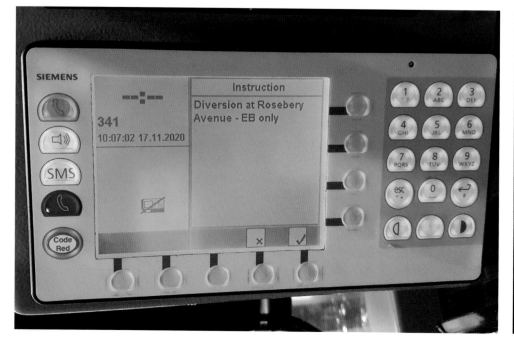